Kevin Garnett: The Inspiring Story of One of Basketball's Greatest Power Forwards

An Unauthorized Biography

By: Clayton Geoffreys

Copyright © 2016 by Calvintir Books, LLC

All rights reserved. Neither this book nor any portion thereof may be reproduced or used in any manner whatsoever without the express written permission. Published in the United States of America.

Disclaimer: The following book is for entertainment and informational purposes only. The information presented is without contract or any type of guarantee assurance. While every caution has been taken to provide accurate and current information, it is solely the reader's responsibility to check all information contained in this article before relying upon it. Neither the author nor publisher can be held accountable for any errors or omissions. Under no circumstances will any legal responsibility or blame be held against the author or publisher for any reparation, damages, or monetary loss due to the information presented, either directly or indirectly. This book is not intended as legal or medical advice. If any such specialized advice is needed, seek a qualified individual for help.

Trademarks are used without permission. Use of the trademark is not authorized by, associated with, or sponsored by the trademark owners. All trademarks and brands used within this book are used with no intent to infringe on the trademark owners and only used for clarifying purposes.

This book is not sponsored by or affiliated with the National Basketball Association, its teams, the players, or anyone involved with them.

Visit my website at www.claytongeoffreys.com
Cover photo by Keith Allison is licensed under CC BY 2.0 / modified from original

Table of Contents

Foreword 1

Introduction 3

Chapter 1: Childhood and Early Life 8

Chapter 2: High School Years......................................11

Chapter 3: Kevin Garnett's NBA Career 14

    Getting Drafted 14

    Rookie Season 17

    All-Star Season and Controversial Contract............21

    1998-99 Lockout Season 29

    Superstardom and First Round Exits.......................34

    MVP Season 46

    The Slow Breakup, the Building Frustration..........56

    The Trade to the Celtics 65

    The New Boston Big Three 69

    The Road to Becoming an NBA Champion 76

    Injury, Missed Title Defense 81

Return to the Finals 85

Battling Against the Newest Big Three 93

The End of an Era and the Trade to Brooklyn 101

Brooklyn Stint 104

Minnesota Homecoming 107

Retirement 113

Chapter 4: Garnett's Personal Life 115

Chapter 5: Garnett's Legacy and Impact on the Game 117

Final Word/About the Author 120

References 123

Foreword

Google "anything is possible" and the results that follow will include something with Kevin Garnett's name attached. Few sports moments since the turn of the millennium have been as monumental as that 2008 NBA Finals moment when the Boston Celtics won the NBA Championship. Kevin Garnett will easily go down as one of the greatest power forwards to play the game of basketball. His high basketball IQ paired with his adept ability to lead teams in practically every statistical category made him the definition of a franchise player. Since jumping into the NBA straight from high school, Garnett has left a deep imprint for future big men to play the game. Even more recently, he has served as an influential mentor for both Karl-Anthony Towns and Andrew Wiggins. Thank you for downloading *Kevin Garnett: The Inspiring Story of One of Basketball's Greatest Power Forwards*. In this unauthorized biography, we will learn Kevin's incredible life story and impact on the game of basketball. Hope you enjoy, and if you do, please do not forget to leave a review!

Also, check out my website at claytongeoffreys.com to join my exclusive list where I let you know about my latest books. To thank you for your purchase, you can go to my site to download a free copy of *33 Life Lessons: Success Principles, Career Advice & Habits of Successful People*. In the book, you will learn from some of the greatest thought leaders of different industries on what it takes to become successful and how to live a great life.

Cheers,

Clayton Geoffreys

Visit me at www.claytongeoffreys.com

Introduction

No single person in the history of the NBA has been as fiery on both ends of the court as Kevin Garnett. Aside from his lone championship, individual accolades, numerous All-Star game appearances, and career milestones, Kevin Garnett (or KG as he is better known) is intensity personified on the basketball court. Whether as a teammate or as a player on the opposing side, KG will always push you to your limit in any manner conceivable and will get into your head both on and off the court. He drives people so hard that he once made his Boston Celtics teammate Glen "Big Baby" Davis cry during a televised game by scolding him on the sidelines after a timeout. Moreover, opposing players tend to get the worst aspects of his intensity because he is a very physical player and is one of the best trash-talkers in the game. He once called opposing forward Charlie Villanueva a "cancer on the team" while defending him. KG has even gone as far as insulting All-Star Carmelo Anthony's wife during a game.

However, it is also KG's intense persona that contributed to his legendary and accomplished career. He is a 15-time NBA All-Star, one-time MVP, one-time Defensive Player of the Year, Olympic gold medalist, an All-NBA team member nine times, a

12-time All-Defensive team member (tied with Kobe Bryant for second of all-time), and above all, an NBA champion. He is also today's longest tenured NBA player and has been with the league since the 1995 season.

While most people remember Garnett for his pre-game head banging ritual on the basket stanchion and for his hard chest pumps, there have also been several memorable moments in KG's career. In 1995, he was the first high school player to be drafted into the NBA within the last 20 years. He was also the MVP of the 2003 All-Star Game held in Atlanta wherein he recorded 37 points and nine boards en route to a Western team victory. In 2008, he made headlines when he was traded to the Boston Celtics, forming a new era Boston Big Three together with Paul Pierce and Ray Allen. And who could ever forget that post-game interview after his Boston Celtics won the NBA Finals in 2008 over the Los Angeles Lakers wherein he shouted to the home crowd and the world that "anything is possible"?

Listed at 6'11" (and probably taller) and 250 lbs., Kevin Garnett was big and strong, both of which are aspects that helped him dominate both the offensive and defensive sides of the court. Because of his height and length, KG has been a steady force in the league ever since he entered the draft in 1995. He has a career average of over 18 points per game spanning 21 years of NBA basketball.

Tall and long players like Kevin McHale, Kareem Abdul-Jabbar, and David Robinson would pivot at the low post, and traditional power forwards like Charles Barkley and Karl Malone made the position fit for bruisers. Kevin Garnett was an innovator and a fundamentally sound big man who initially earned his living by making midrange jump shots and skillful finishes at the basket.

Garnett could also dribble the ball down the court after a rebound for a breakaway play. And for a man his size, Kevin Garnett was always one of the most gifted passers at the power forward position in the history of the NBA. As far as the word "conventional" goes, KG started out as someone that went against the norms of his size and playing position.

It was only when he beefed up his body that he began to bang down low with the big men at the post. Not only was Kevin Garnett tall, but he also had long arms, with a wingspan of about 7'5". This helped him grab a lot of rebounds for a 10.2 career rebounding average, helped him to see over defenses to make assist passes, and to block shots on the defensive end (which is a side to his game he is well known for, on top of his scoring abilities).

Despite being a physical specimen and talented superstar, it took Kevin Garnett 13 seasons and two hall-of-fame teammates to win a championship. Nevertheless, he is a perennial winner and a unique basketball player. He is an innovator and became a standard for many tall and long big men in today's game. KG did things no other 7-footer in league history would have dared to do. He was not only an innovator as far as far as playing style was concerned, but was also one of the first to ever show a palpable level of intensity and passion on the basketball court.

Garnett became the prototype and standard for big men such as Chris Bosh and Anthony Davis. Even Kevin Durant, who stands almost 7 feet tall, would not be seen handling the ball and taking jump shots if Kevin Garnett had not paved the way for younger players. And, in the twilight of Garnett's career, young Timberwolves big man Karl-Anthony Towns was lucky to be under the tutelage of one of the best big men to ever play the game.

Not only was Kevin a pioneer as a basketball player, but he was also a pioneer for other high school stars to follow. Since 1975, no high school player was ever drafted in the NBA. As LeBron James recounted, Kevin Garnett (and Kobe Bryant) paved the way for prep-to-pro superstars like himself.[i] While younger players may emulate and pattern their games after Garnett's, and while many talented high school players followed his footsteps onto the NBA hardwood, we may never again see a player who is as intense, passionate, and as fiery as Kevin Garnett is.

Chapter 1: Childhood and Early Life

Kevin Garnett was born in Greenville, South Carolina on May 19, 1976, to parents Shirley Garnett and O'Lewis McCullough. Kevin's parents met because O'Lewis frequently played in local basketball leagues and Shirley was fond of watching the game. However, they never got married officially, even after Kevin was born. O'Lewis abandoned Shirley during Kevin's early infancy. Thus, Shirley had no choice but to raise Kevin as a single parent with the help of her eldest daughter, Sonya.[ii]

Shirley had to work two jobs to make ends meet as raising her children, Sonya, Kevin, and youngest daughter Ashley became increasingly complicated. His father O'Lewis, though he sent money for child support, did not do enough to contribute to raising KG. However absent O'Lewis was in his life, Kevin does admit that his father, who played center despite being only 6'4", was one of the reasons he got into basketball. Kevin apparently got his basketball talents from his father.

Growing up was difficult for the young Garnett. Aside from having no father figure and financial difficulties, he lived in a troubled neighborhood in Greenville. He also did not enjoy holidays such as Christmas and Halloween because Shirley was a devout Jehovah's Witness. On the bright side, he did have many friends and relatives living nearby in the neighborhood, including his grandparents from his father's side.

When Shirley later married Ernest Irby just as Kevin turned seven years old, it looked like things would take a turn for the better for their family. When he turned 12, they moved from Greenville to nearby Mauldin where Kevin spent most of his childhood and teenage years. It was there in Mauldin, during middle school, where KG started to fall in love with basketball.

Kevin Garnett turned to basketball as his solace and for retreat whenever he wanted to get things off his mind. He would often sneak out late at night to play ball at a nearby park whenever he could not sleep. Like most kids who grew up in the 80's, Kevin was in awe of the Showtime era of the Los Angeles Lakers led by Magic Johnson. This made him try to pattern his game after Johnson, and this is one of the reasons why he had the grace and skills of a guard even as a big man in the NBA.

Though he was living a more comfortable life than before, and though he already had a father figure, Garnett wanted someone who would help him develop his basketball skills. Sadly, his stepfather Ernest was not a big fan of sports and initially wanted Kevin to focus intently on his studies. This persisted as a point of contention with his stepfather. With no parental figure to help and support him with his dream of making it to the NBA, he turned to his friends. That was when he met and befriended a boy named Jamie Peters. They would often play at local ballparks and against bigger and older teenagers. This experience helped shape Kevin as a basketball player as he was forced to toughen up and hone his skills to stand a chance against the older teenagers. [iii]

Chapter 2: High School Years

Kevin Garnett never played organized basketball until his freshman year at Mauldin High School where he averaged 12.5 points, 14 rebounds, and an incredible seven blocks per game. As a freshman, he stood 6'6" and was used primarily as a defender and rebounder.[iv]

Kevin continued to hone and further develop his game in his sophomore year. He credited his AAU team during the previous summer for continuing to help him improve his skills and confidence. He wowed his coach in his sophomore season by expanding his offensive repertoire. He started demanding the ball at the low post, which was something he rarely did the previous year.

In his 3rd year at Mauldin high school, he averaged 27 points, 17 rebounds, and seven blocks per game on his way to a state championship. It was then that Garnett started getting the attention of scouts. Even at that young age, colleges already began lining up to recruit the up and coming phenom.[v]

However, before he could get into his senior year, Garnett was involved in an incident concerning a white student allegedly getting assaulted by several black students, including Kevin. He was arrested and charged with second-degree lynching. Luckily, he was released on bail and charges against him were dropped. Even now, KG defends himself and maintains that he had no hand in the incident.[vi]

The nature of the event, being an alleged racial dispute, combined with Kevin Garnett's status as a basketball prodigy led to statewide coverage and scrutiny of the story. Due to the controversy and fear that his reputation as a player and a person was besmirched by the incident, Kevin turned to basketball and focused on his AAU team to get everything off of his mind. During the Nike summer camp, Kevin made the decision to move to Chicago and transfer to Farragut Academy to play basketball during his senior year.

Together with his friend Ronnie Fields, Garnett transformed Farragut Academy into a powerhouse in Chicago. Farragut seemed unstoppable with a record of 28 wins against only two losses, while Garnett himself was averaging 25 points, 18 rebounds, almost seven assists, and 6.5 swats a game, quickly on his way to being named by USA Today as the National High School Player of the Year. Farragut Academy won the city title and made it all the way to the state quarterfinals.

At the 18th anniversary of the McDonald's All-American Game, Kevin was named to play together with future NBA superstar

Vince Carter and future teammates Paul Pierce and Stephon Marbury. At the conclusion of the game, Garnett literally and figuratively stood tall above all the rest as the Most Outstanding Player with 18 points, 11 rebounds, four assists, and three blocks.

Now that he was living and playing in a bigger city, there was more opportunity for exposure on the part of the young Kevin Garnett. While Kevin certainly wanted to go to college and play in the NCAA, fate decided otherwise. KG initially failed to reach the requisite score on the SAT to be eligible to play at the collegiate level. At the time, it seemed to him that the most feasible decision was to go straight to the NBA. Still trying his luck, he took the test a fourth time.

Kevin got a call from his coach at Farragut Academy telling him that he had finally reached the required score on the SAT, which meant that he was now eligible to play in the NCAA. However, it was too late, and Kevin Garnett had moved on to greener pastures. He was already a member of the Minnesota Timberwolves, drafted 5th overall in the 1995 NBA Draft.[vii]

Chapter 3: Kevin Garnett's NBA Career

Getting Drafted

Kevin Garnett was an intriguing prospect coming into the 1995 NBA Draft. The NBA at that time was run by powerful and bruising big men like Shaquille O'Neal, Hakeem Olajuwon, Patrick Ewing, Karl Malone, and David Robinson. Any successful team other than the Chicago Bulls in that era of basketball had a huge center in the middle to punish opposing teams inside the paint. The traditional big man was the very essence needed for a team to win games back then.

As tall as Garnett was, he was not built the same way as those giants were. There was no way a skinny teenager could hold his own against them in the paint. Here was a lanky, scrawny kid who stood at above 6'10" and had arms so long they could block out the sun. He was a teenager and still growing. However, back then, Kevin Garnett did not win games or put up points by dominating his opposing big man. He did not play with his back to the basket to try and put his defenders through punishing bruises. Simply put, KG was a lot different back then. The beauty of Garnett's game was that he moved with the skill and grace of a guard, and had a smooth-looking jump shot. At nearly 7 feet tall, Kevin Garnett can bring the ball down the court better than smaller players while also hitting jumpers at a higher rate than guards. At the same time, he could swat shots and rebound the ball like centers his size would do, but could also trigger the fast break himself and run the floor as quick as the smaller forwards and guards.

Athletically, Kevin Garnett was miles ahead of his peers and competitors back at the high school level, or even if he had decided to go to college. Not only was KG taller and longer than his opposition, but he was also faster, quicker, and agiler than any other big man in the preparatory ranks in the country back then. He was a load to handle as far as athleticism was concerned. [viii]

But while Garnett had the superior size and athletic ability in college to blow past his defenders and finish with highlight dunks in the paint, the young teenager's go-to move was his turnaround jumper. Even back then, KG was already able to master that virtually unguardable move that high school players were always seen struggling to try and contest him whenever he turned his right shoulder.[viii]

Given the fact that Kevin Garnett was an offensive blessing and an attractive prospect for a go-to guy in the future, what was an underrated, yet ever important part of his game coming out of high school was his defense. KG was long and tall. He could have easily swatted away shots back in high school. However, it was always his desire to play hard on defense and be virtually everywhere on the floor that made him a unique defensive prospect.

As the Minnesota Timberwolves owned the fifth overall pick, then-Timberwolves vice president of basketball operations Kevin McHale decided to choose the best possible player available to be the cornerstone of his rebuilt Minnesota team. A legendary big man himself, McHale was always impressed by Kevin Garnett's abilities. He flourished in special workouts designed for guards and smaller players, but could still protect the paint using his size and height.

John Hammond, then-Milwaukee Bucks general manager, remembered how he was awed the first time he put Garnett in a workout. He was amazed at how KG could put the ball on the floor, dribble with flair, and still finish strong at the basket.

However promising of an athlete and prospect Kevin was, many, including McHale, thought he was a risky gamble because he was untested in the collegiate ranks where most of his draft mates had made impacts and had successful careers. John Nash, the Washington Bullets (now Wizards) general manager at that time, recounted that the Bullets executives told him not to draft

Kevin as the fourth overall pick because they did not feel like it was a good choice to pick an unproven player right out of high school. Thus, prospects Joe Smith, Antonio McDyess, Jerry Stackhouse, and Rasheed Wallace were respectively the top four picks since they were thought to be more proven and polished players than Kevin Garnett.

With the best possible choices now unavailable, Kevin McHale and the Timberwolves turned their attention to the lanky teenager and grabbed him as the fifth overall pick in the 1995 NBA Draft. KG sealed the deal by signing his first NBA contract worth $5.6 million over three years. "Da Kid," as he was called at that time, officially became the first prep-to-pro player to sign with an NBA team since 1975. The last person to do it was Daryl Dawkins two decades before.[ix]

Rookie Season

Even though the Minnesota Timberwolves was a rebuilding team during Garnett's rookie season, they already had seasoned big men in Christian Laettner and offseason acquisition Tom Gugliotta. Moreover, then-head coach Bill Blair did not want to rush Kevin's development and opted to relegate him to come off the bench to back up Laettner and Gugliotta. Because of that, KG never saw much time or touches.

Garnett made his NBA debut on November 3, 1995, scoring only 8 points on a perfect shooting night in a loss for the Wolves. He would only play 16 minutes in that game before seeing only 11 in the next match. KG would not score in that game. Nevertheless, Da Kid would play 26 minutes in his third game while putting up 8 points and five rebounds.

Kevin Garnett, for the very first time in his career, would crack double-digit scoring on November 15. In that loss to the San Antonio Spurs, KG had 19 points and 8 rebounds, 7 of which came from the offensive end. It would take more than a month until Garnett would score in double digits again as his coach seldom utilized his services on the offensive end. In that December 17 loss to the Philadelphia 76ers, he had 12 points and five rebounds in only 16 minutes. Five days later, in another loss, he would score 17 points on 6 out of 9 shooting from the floor.

However, things were not going according to plan, and Kevin McHale had to shake up his coaching staff midseason by replacing Blair with a new head coach in Phil "Flip" Saunders. Flip Saunders brought new life and hope for the struggling franchise. He saw KG's potential and decided to turn his attention to the young and developing forward. Kevin was then injected into the starting lineup under Saunder's system where he flourished.

Kevin Garnett would make his first ever start on January 30, 1996. Though he did not immediately flourish, KG's potential was apparent as he grabbed 11 rebounds for his first double-digit rebounding night. On February 7, he would have his first ever double-double when the Timberwolves lost to the Portland Trailblazers. Kevin Garnett had 12 points and 12 rebounds in that milestone night.

In what was a career best in minutes for him at that point in his career, KG had 16 points, 15 rebounds, and two blocks in 43 minutes of action in a narrow loss to the Chicago Bulls. On February 19, Garnett then started a three-game streak of double-doubles along with starting a 31-game double-digit scoring streak. Late in February, he would break 20 points for the first time when he made 10 of his 16 field goals in a loss to the Bulls. As Kevin Garnett was rising, fourth-year veteran big man Christian Laettner was not fond of the direction the team was taking and how Garnett was getting more touches at the offensive end. It became evident that the two could not coexist when Garnett and Laettner were seen arguing in a team huddle during a timeout in a game against Washington. The veteran player was upset that Garnett would not pass him the ball unless he was open. He even went to the media and openly admitted that he wanted rookies and younger players to "shut up" and leave it to the coaching staff and the more experienced players to "take care of the team" because the veterans and the coaching staff "knew a lot more" than the rookies.[x] Adding fuel to the fire, Flip Saunders said that there might have been players on the roster who were jealous of the attention Garnett was receiving and admitted that he was "better than anyone on the team," including Laettner.

With the new coaching staff and the developing Kevin Garnett not seeing eye-to-eye with his older teammates, Kevin McHale had no choice but to ship Laettner over to Atlanta in the middle of the season in exchange for the Hawks' Andrew Lang and Spud Webb. With the frontcourt now open, Kevin Garnett now had all the opportunities and tools he needed to flourish under Saunders and begin to take over the team, and eventually, take the league by storm.

Continuing his streak of double-digit scoring, Garnett scored a new career high of 23 points along with nine rebounds in a loss to the New York Knicks on March 13. Nearly two weeks later, KG had his best game as a rookie when he had 33 points on 14 out of 21 shooting in a narrow loss to the Boston Celtics. He also added eight rebounds, four assists, and three blocks in that game. Da Kid ended his rookie season with 14 points and 11 rebounds in his 80th outing that year.

As the regular season ended, it was Garnett and center Tom Gugliotta who bore the scoring and offensive load for the young Minnesota squad. At the end of his first season, Kevin Garnett averaged 10.4 points, 6.3 rebounds, 1.1 steals, and 1.6 blocks, making his way to getting voted into the All-Rookie Second team. Meanwhile, the Timberwolves suffered a losing season, winning only 26 games and not making the playoffs.

Despite the early struggles and lack of playing time for Kevin Garnett, the one thing that was clear was that the then-19-year-old teenager was destined for great things to come for the NBA. That was shown by his late season surge when the Timberwolves turned their attention to the budding young man that played all facets of the game at a high level.

All-Star Season and Controversial Contract

The second half of the 1995-96 season was a sign of good things to come for a rising Minnesota Timberwolves team, especially with Kevin Garnett manning both the offense and defense of the team simultaneously. Before the 1996 season got started, team executives were intent on improving and augmenting the team by adding a running mate for Garnett.

On the day of the 1996 NBA Draft, the Timberwolves made a move that would send newly drafted rookie (and future Celtic teammate) Ray Allen, the fifth pick of the draft, to the Milwaukee Bucks. The trade was in exchange for 4th overall pick Stephon Marbury, who already had ties with Garnett, having exchanged several phone calls way before their respective NBA years.

As an accomplished point guard in the collegiate ranks, Marbury was a good complementary piece for KG. Garnett now had someone who could pass him the ball on explosive drives and in transition, and someone who could catch and shoot on kickoff passes from the interior. Marbury was also a significant upgrade for the Timberwolves that lacked help from the backcourt.

With an improved supporting cast around him, KG started from where he left off the previous season, albeit on a better note as far as victories were concerned. Garnett opened the season with a win against the Spurs. He had 17 points, nine rebounds, six assists, three steals, and four blocks for a well-rounded stat line. On November 12, he had an even better outing when he had 20 points, 11 rebounds, five assists, four steals, and three blocks in the Timberwolves' win over the Portland Trailblazers.

Though it came at a loss, KG had a new career high in rebounds on November 27 against the Seattle SuperSonics. Garnett had 17 rebounds to go along with 21 points, seven assists, three steals, and two blocks. That performance was already Garnett's sixth double-double for the year, though he had only played 13 games up to that point.

In his first game of 1997, Kevin Garnett had a career night on the defensive end when he recorded eight blocks in a win over the Boston Celtics. In the following night in a win over the Milwaukee Bucks, KG did it again. Along with his eight blocks, Garnett had 22 points, 13 rebounds, and four assists. In the last five games including those back-to-back defensive performances from Kevin Garnett, he had already compiled a total of 29 rejections.

While defense was probably the best facet of Kevin Garnett's game, he would prove that he was also a growing offensive threat when he recorded four consecutive games of scoring at least 20 points in January. And in the twilight days of the month, Garnett had two 30-point outings. He had 32 on 12 out of 25 shooting in a loss to the Portland Trailblazers, and on the final day of January, Garnett had 30 points in a win over the Spurs.

Because of how quickly KG was rising through the ranks while captivating fans and coaches alike with his all-around performances, Da Kid was awarded a recognition reserved for the best performances of the season. In only his second season and at barely even 21 years old, Kevin Garnett managed to make the Western Conference All-Star team together with teammate and Timberwolves leading scorer and rebounder Tom Gugliotta. At that time, he was the youngest player to make an All-Star team since Magic Johnson made it back in 1980.

In the same season, the T-Wolves drastically improved. The franchise found new life from the energy and chemistry that was evidently oozing out of their young players Kevin Garnett and Stephon Marbury. The inside-outside combination together with a few pick and roll/pop connections between the two led people to think that they may be seeing the newest versions of John Stockton and Karl Malone.[xi] Current Minnesota head coach Sam Mitchell even believed that the Garnett-Marbury duo was an even better combination than Stockton and Malone because Marbury was a much better scorer than Stockton, compounded by the fact that Garnett is also a better defender than Malone.[xii]

At the end of the regular season, the Timberwolves surprised the whole league and improved by 14 wins on their way to the playoffs with a 40-42 record. Kevin Garnett drastically improved in every facet of his game, averaging 17 points, eight rebounds, 3.1 assists, 1.7 steals, and 2.1 blocks. His backcourt counterpart Stephon Marbury averaged almost 16 points and nearly eight assists per game for a very successful rookie season.

While being a season revelation, the Timberwolves were not content with just making the playoffs. Like every other team, they had the intention of winning the NBA title. However, the intention remained a dream at the time as they met fierce competition in the first round, facing a powerhouse Houston Rockets team. The Houston Rockets had championship experience after having won back-to-back titles in 1994 and 1995. They also had three superstars led by two-time champion Hakeem Olajuwon, former MVP Charles Barkley, and highflying volume scorer Clyde Drexler. As everyone expected, the powerhouse and veteran Rockets team swept the young and inexperienced Garnett-led Timberwolves in three games.

Kevin Garnett's rookie contract was about to expire at the end of his 3rd NBA season. The Timberwolves offered him a $102 million contract extension for the following six seasons. In an unprecedented move, the young Garnett declined the massive contract extension in the hopes of landing a bigger deal with one of the big market teams in Los Angeles or New York.

Afraid of losing their prized young player to a bigger and brighter market team, the Minnesota Timberwolves would put all of their eggs in a basket for the developing Kevin Garnett. In an additional unprecedented move, the Minnesota Timberwolves had no choice but to offer KG a 6-year, $126 million contract extension, which the latter happily accepted. This contract, at the time, was the largest contract in the history of not just the NBA, but of professional sports in general.[xiii]

The record-breaking deal not only drew the attention of people around the world, but it also drew the ire and criticisms from players and coaches alike. Here was a young and talented player who had a lot of superstar potential in him. He had not proven himself on the NBA stage. He was just a one-time All-Star. He had not won any major individual awards, nor did he have the pleasure of being picked for an All-NBA team.

Moreover, the Timberwolves under KG's leadership had not seen any success as a franchise. They had not had a winning record, nor had they gone past the first round of the playoffs, or won an NBA title. Even Michael Jordan, in all his NBA greatness and championships, had not earned a total of $126 million in his whole NBA career. Even Shaquille O'Neal, who was a proven and more established dominant force in the NBA at that time, signed a contract with the Lakers for $6 million less than Garnett's. Thus, people were led to believe that Garnett was a selfish and self-centered player who only played for the money.

Minnesota was intent on silencing the doubts and criticisms of the contract by making the team more successful with a newly extended Kevin Garnett as the cornerstone. They surrounded KG and Marbury with a complementary veteran in Terry Porter as well as retaining key pieces such as Tom Gugliotta and Sam Mitchell.

The team enjoyed a relatively successful 1997-98 season while Kevin Garnett continued to perform exceptionally. On top of that, the developing young superstar was still getting better and better. KG would start that season with a win against the Golden State Warriors while putting up a terrific stat line of 25 points, 11 rebounds, seven assists, and six blocks. Two weeks later, he would pull down a new career high of 20 rebounds along with 20 points for his first 20-20 game.

It would not take long for such a gifted 7-foot passing big man like Kevin Garnett to get his first triple-double. On January 3, 1998, KG would have 18 points, 13 rebounds, and ten assists in a blowout win over the Denver Nuggets. Three games later, he completed a six-game streak of double-doubles as the solid core of Garnett, Marbury, and Gugliotta led the team to a then-franchise record seven straight victories.

Those kinds of performances catapulted KG to a starting spot for the Western Conference All-Stars. Not too shabby himself, Gugliotta also saw another All-Star caliber year. However, he saw his season ending with a severe knee injury. Nevertheless, the Wolves rallied to Kevin Garnett's ferocity as the young power forward averaged 18 points, 9.6 rebounds, and 4.2 assists at season's end while leading the team to a playoff-qualifying record of 45 wins and 37 losses, the first ever winning season in Minnesota Timberwolves history. In the same season, Garnett achieved personal milestones as he broke the Wolves' single-season record for double-doubles, minutes played, and total rebounds. While only in his third year in the league and despite the young history of the Minnesota Timberwolves, one could argue that KG had already become the franchise's best player ever.

In consecutive seasons, the Timberwolves faced another Western Conference powerhouse veteran team. This time, it was the Seattle Supersonics (now Oklahoma City Thunder) led by defensive stalwart and certified superstar point guard Gary Payton.

Unlike the previous season, the Garnett-led Wolves gave the Sonics a tough fight that ultimately resulted in a do-or-die game five. KG's best performance was when he led his team to a 2-1 lead over the Sonics by posting 19 points, eight rebounds, six assists, and three blocks in Game 3 of the series. They would almost upset Seattle when they lost Game 4 by only four points. To their dismay, the Timberwolves lost the series to Seattle, but not without a franchise milestone, with the two wins they had becoming the first playoff wins in Minnesota Timberwolves history. In a season full of career milestones, dunk, and block highlights for Kevin Garnett, the biggest highlight of his third NBA season remained to be the $126 million contract that triggered a downward spiral for not only the Timberwolves but for the whole NBA.

1998-99 Lockout Season

Many attributed the 1998-99 lockout season to the unprecedented and ultra-lucrative contracts that several NBA players signed. Players such as Alonzo Mourning and Shaquille O'Neal minted contracts just above the $100 million range. However, none of those contracts were nearly as lucrative as the one that Kevin Garnett signed. Even Timberwolves Owner Glen Taylor believes that KG's contract played the biggest hand in triggering the lockout.

The huge amount of cash that certain superstar players were signing for made several owners and players alike feel that the salary cap system at that time was broken and that changes needed to be made to the system to protect both owner profits and player salaries at the same time. Ron Klempner of the NBPA said that Garnett's contract was the "ammunition the owners needed" to trigger a change in the system. Indeed it was, and it became the main topic in union talks.

As owner Glen Taylor recounts, he believed that the contract offered to Garnett was to give hope to the Minnesota Timberwolves fans that change was coming, that they needed to hold on to their support of the struggling franchise, and that they would soon become successful with Kevin Garnett. However, he never believed that the contract was a good decision as far as business was concerned.[xiv]

Due to the lockout, there was a stoppage in the NBA. It was late January of 1999 when the NBA began the new season when an agreement between the owners and players union was finally struck. The season was shortened to 50 games, and there was no All-Star Weekend. The new Collective Bargaining Agreement (CBA) between the players and owners featured several changes that all stemmed from Garnett's contract.

First of all, the initial rookie contract was extended from three years to five. This was seen as a preventive measure against teams signing fresh sophomore players for hundred million dollar contracts. The second featured change set a maximum amount that any player could sign to, regardless of years played and stature in the NBA.

On top of the lockout, the Minnesota Timberwolves also had troubles as a franchise coming into the lockout-shortened season. First, the team let Tom Gugliotta sign with the Phoenix Suns to save money from the lockout and to have enough space to resign Marbury. Second and worst of all, Kevin Garnett's contract got Stephon Marbury jealous.

Team ownership was so intent on keeping Garnett that they forgot about Marbury. Under the new CBA, the most that Marbury could get out of the Timberwolves was a contract extension for six years at $71 million. He did not want to take less money than KG did because he was just as talented and crucial to the team as his teammate was. In the end, Minnesota moved Stephon Marbury in a three-team trade that sent Marbury to the New Jersey Nets while Minnesota got a replacement guard in Terrell Brandon as well as two future draft picks.

Without their former leading scorer Gugliotta and explosive guard Marbury, it was left to Kevin Garnett to pick up the scoring load tenfold. Not only was he leading the team in scoring for the first time in his career, but he was also grabbing rebounds more than he ever did as his frontcourt buddy was off in Phoenix with a better contract offer.

Garnett would initially find that life as a lone star on the Minnesota Timberwolves was tough. The lack of a good supporting cast of scorers and the long layoff from any basketball activities took a toll on Garnett in the first few games of the season. Always known as an efficient shooter, KG combined for 21 out of 70 from the field in his first three games of the season as defenders keyed in on him.

However, KG would eventually break out of the slump to post monster numbers that the world had gotten used to seeing from him. On February 21, 1999, Garnett had 22 points, 19 rebounds, seven assists, five steals, and two blocks in a win against the Sacramento Kings. That was the third game of what would become a five-game streak of assisting on at least six baskets. At that point, KG had already grown in his secondary role as a playmaker.

Kevin Garnett would play all facets of the game exceptionally well throughout the season as he acted as the team's best scorer, defender, and rebounder in addition to being one of the better playmakers on the team. Though he would not record a triple-double that season, Garnett narrowly missed several instances. On March 16, KG had 21 points, 11 rebounds, and nine assists in a defeat versus the Los Angeles Lakers. Twelve days later, he had 16 points, 18 rebounds, and nine assists in a loss to the Milwaukee Bucks. Then, on April 12 when the season was nearing its end, Garnett recorded 21 points, nine rebounds, and 11 assists against the Houston Rockets.

Despite the fact that KG had been an All-Star twice in four years, the 1999 season was the breakout season for KG. It was his first 20-10 season and the first time he had experienced carrying a team on his back as a lone star. He averaged almost 21 points per game, ten rebounds, and 4.3 assists to go along with 1.8 blocks. He was also recognized as one of the NBA's fifteen best players and was named a member of the All-NBA Third Team.

As spectacular as KG's season was, his shorthanded team struggled to make the playoffs. They barely made it to the post-season tournament as the 8th seeded Western Conference team. For the 3rd straight post-season, they faced another loaded team. They had to try their luck against what would become the eventual champion San Antonio Spurs team with an imposing frontline of former MVP David Robinson and fellow up-and-coming player Tim Duncan who would, in a few years, become one of his biggest rivals for the crown of the generation's best power forward.

KG and the T-Wolves only managed to win only a single game against the much stronger Spurs team. That was in Game 2 of the series when Garnett posted 23 points, 12 rebounds, six assists, three steals, and two blocks to lead his team to tie the much stronger lineup. However, the twin tower frontcourt of the Spurs proved too much for KG as San Antonio went on to win Games 3 and 4. Kevin Garnett could not break out of the first round of the playoffs for the third straight season.

Superstardom and First Round Exits

Though Minnesota was unsuccessful in winning a title or at least going deep into the playoffs the previous season, there was one bright spot that proved certain—it was that Kevin Garnett was a legitimate NBA superstar. At 23 years old, he was still young concerning age but already had ample NBA years and talent in his belt to lead a team on his back.

Still leading the same pack of resilient Wolves, Garnett started the 1999-2000 season with seven consecutive double-double performances as he established his name as a premier young superstar in the league. He even had three straight 30-10 games to start the season. In one of the team's two losses during those seven games, KG even put up 23 points and 20 rebounds versus the LA Clippers.

In the middle of December, Kevin Garnett would post monstrous numbers again as he led his team to five straight victories. While averaging at least 20 points and 13 rebounds in that stretch, Garnett was also making plays and defending at a high level. It was also during that stretch when he had his second 20-20 game of the season when he had 26 points and 23 rebounds together with seven assists and four blocks versus the Orlando Magic.

On January 17, 2000, KG would have a new career best in points when he defeated the Indiana Pacers with his 37 points along with 13 rebounds and seven assists. In the next game, he again had at least 30 points and would lead his team to five consecutive wins for another occasion that season. It was those kinds of performances and leadership qualities that led the Wolves to wins and catapulted Kevin Garnett to a third All-Star appearance.

At the end of it all, Garnett posted highs in points, rebounds, assists. He normed 22.9 points, 11.8 rebounds, and five assists all year long while adding 1.5 steals and 1.6 blocks. He also led the Minnesota Timberwolves to their first ever 50-win season.

Kevin Garnett did not do the task on his own, however. He had help in the form of point guard Terrell Brandon who continued to play like an All-Star. Rookie Wally Szczerbiak also had a fantastic first season for the T-Wolves by chipping in much-needed points from the perimeter. Best of all, they had the veteran presence of Malik Sealy, who was one of KG's favorite players. Garnett was also elevated to the All-NBA First Team. And as a testament to his tenacious defense, he was also named to the All-Defensive First Team.

However, a hopeful season was shattered when Sealy was killed in an automobile accident on May 20, 2000. The death of one of their veteran leaders devastated KG and the rest of the Minnesota squad. They could not get past the first round for a fourth straight season at the hands of the eventual Western Conference Finalists the Portland Trailblazers, headlined by six-time champion Scottie Pippen and versatile big man Rasheed Wallace. Nevertheless, KG posted a new milestone when he had 23 points, 13 rebounds, and ten assists in Game 3 of that series. That was the Timberwolves' only win against the Blazers.

As the saying goes, basketball never stops. After another unsuccessful season, Kevin Garnett was chosen as a member of the USA Men's Basketball Team in the 2000 Olympic Games in Sydney, Australia. He joined fellow young All-Stars Vince Carter, Ray Allen, and Antonio McDyess. Garnett averaged almost 11 points per game together with nine rebounds in a decisive role for Team USA's gold medal victory.

The Team USA experience and gold medal victory proved to be an irreplaceable experience for the veteran forward as he continued his stellar play the following season. In the 2000-01 season, he averaged 22 points, 11.4 rebounds, five assists, 1.3 steals, and 1.8 blocks per game for another All-Star, All-NBA, and Defensive team selection season. In the same season, he also reached a milestone of 291 straight double-digit games.

The Minnesota Timberwolves looked to improve on their previous season's record. They added a talented point guard in Chauncey Billups to serve a backup role to Terrell Brandon. Szczerbiak also improved his scoring numbers. However, the team faced more controversy even before the season started. The league penalized the team for the illegal signing of Joe Smith, who was the first overall pick in Garnett's draft class. The T-Wolves were stripped of three future first round picks. They also lost general manager Kevin McHale, who was banned from the NBA for a year.

However, life went on for the Minnesota Timberwolves and Kevin Garnett. Still leading the charge for the Wolves, KG had 13 double-double performances in his first 20 games of the season. In those 20 games, Garnett only scored below 20 points once and was growing to become more consistent on the offensive end. He would lead the Wolves to a 12-8 record in those 20 outings.

On December 15, 2000, Kevin Garnett had his first triple-double of the season when he posted 26 points, 13 rebounds, and ten assists on his way to a win over the Detroit Pistons. And just a night later, he was not done with his ways of posting monstrous numbers. In a win over the Indiana Pacers, KG had 34 points and 20 rebounds for his first 30-20 game.

It would take nearly two months later for Kevin Garnett to put up another career night. Scoring a new high in points, KG had 40 markers to go along with seven rebounds and six assists in an easy win over the Sacramento Kings. He would play only 34 minutes that game while shooting 17 out of 22 from the field and a rare 2 out of 2 from the three-point area. KG would again see his name on the list of All-Stars.

Shortly after the All-Star Weekend, Kevin Garnett went on to compile ten straight games of double-double performances. In the middle of that, he even had a triple-double game in a win against the Detroit Pistons when he posted 18 points, ten rebounds, and ten assists. He nearly had his third triple-double when he had 26 points, 16 rebounds, and nine assists in a win against the Sonics. And on two other occasions during that streak, Garnett had eight assists.

As the season ended, the Wolves seemed a lesser version of their previous selves. Nevertheless, the team still managed to win a majority of their games to make the playoffs with Kevin Garnett serving as a scorer, rebounder, facilitator, and defender. With a low seeded record of 47-35, Garnett and company would once again face a tough playoffs opponent in the first round. It was a rematch against the Spurs with a featured rivalry of the league's best power forwards—Kevin Garnett versus Tim Duncan.

The series started with Kevin Garnett performing well in Game 1. He had 25 points, 13 rebounds, and six assists. However, Tim Duncan bested him individually by posting 33 points and 15 rebounds. The Spurs would take Game 1. Though Garnett outplayed Duncan in Game 2, the Spurs would again win that bout to take a 2-0 lead.

As he always did, Kevin Garnett refused to get swept by willing his team to a victory in Game 3. He had 22 points and eight rebounds while limiting Timmy due to foul trouble. Once again, however, Duncan's Spurs won the bout and edged out the T-Wolves three games to one by taking Game 4. This was the team's fifth straight first round exit.

Another disappointing season did not hinder KG from further improving his game or from trying to do everything for his team.

As much as Minnesota wanted to put a ring on the finger of their franchise player, the illegal signing of Joe Smith the previous year still haunted them as they were stripped of three first round draft picks. Thus, they could not improve the team with younger talent. Working with what they had, KG and the T-Wolves still managed to win games the next season.[xv]

When the league began allowing zone defenses, Flip Saunders experimented with the lineup as well as with team strategies. He would sometimes relegate the highly versatile Kevin Garnett to the small forward position. After all, KG could move like a guard and could shoot far out on the perimeter. The move proved to be successful as Garnett would explore match-up problems on the offensive end by posting up and shooting over smaller defenders and by stretching defenses with his perimeter shooting. On the defensive end, Garnett's height and lateral movement coupled with the zone defense disrupted opposing offenses.

More evidence of the success was shown when the Timberwolves won their first six games of the season. In what was the closest win the Wolves had in those six games, KG had 37 points and 12 rebounds. He was also instrumental in helping his team win by 53 points against the Chicago Bulls on November 8 for the Wolves' fifth straight win of the season.

One of Kevin Garnett's best stretches of the season was early in December when he led his team to six consecutive wins of double-digit advantages. In the final win of that streak, Garnett had 29 points, eight assists, and a then-career and franchise high of 24 rebounds. Five days later on December 19, he had another 20-rebound night when he pulled down 21 boards in addition to the 20 points, seven assists, and five blocks that he had in a narrow loss to the New Jersey Nets.

Kevin Garnett would prove his leadership skills to be unquestionable as he led his team to another good winning streak. He and the Timberwolves started the year 2002 right by winning nine straight games. KG had seven double-doubles in that streak while nearly posting triple-doubles again several times during that run.

Right after the All-Star break, Kevin Garnett signified that he was back to work by putting up 33 points, 13 rebounds, six assists, two steals, and two blocks in a win over the Phoenix Suns. From then until the end of the season, Garnett would pile up double-doubles in all but four of his final set of games. On March 1, he even had his third 20-20 game of the season when he posted 23 points and 22 rebounds in a win over the New Jersey Nets.

For the fifth season in a row, KG was an All-Star and averaged 21 points, 12 rebounds, 5.2 assists, 1.6 blocks, and 1.2 steals. For the third straight season, he went 20-10-5 in the three most important statistical categories putting him in elite company. His play also earned him another All-NBA Second Team selection and another appearance in the All-Defensive First Team, which all led to a 50-win season for the Timberwolves franchise notwithstanding the season-ending injury to starting point guard Terrell Brandon.

Again, Kevin Garnett's ability to lead a team to victory was questioned in the playoffs. They faced an equally young Dallas Mavericks team led by ultra-talented point guard Steve Nash and equally versatile big man Dirk Nowitzki, who would become another of Garnett's rivals at the power forward position for years to come. What seemed like an equal matchup turned upside-down for the Timberwolves as the Mavs swept them in three games. It was not even because of a lack of effort on Garnett's part as the superstar big man put up 24 points, nearly 19 rebounds, and five assists in those three games. For the sixth straight season, Kevin Garnett faced a first round playoff exit.

All the criticism he received only fueled Kevin Garnett to work on his game even harder. He was intent on being better on both offense and defense. He wanted to become more aggressive and more intense than he had ever been. He then worked harder than ever in the offseason on both his game and body. He started to beef up to become stronger. The skinny and lanky 19-year-old kid was no more.

A beefier and bigger Kevin Garnett started the season strong by piling up a triple-double in just his second game. He had 23 points, 14 rebounds, and ten assists in a win over the Orlando Magic. He then proceeded to start the 2002-03 season with nine straight double-doubles. In one of those games, which was a win against the Milwaukee Bucks, KG had 28 points, 24 rebounds, and six assists. Twelve days later on November 19, 2003, he had another 20-rebound game when he grabbed 22 boards along with 34 markers and six dimes in a victory over the Memphis Grizzlies. Just over a week later, he had his second triple-double of the season in a win against the Kings. Garnett had 20 points, 13 rebounds, and ten assists on that night. One of the criticisms Garnett had in the past was that he would often relegate scoring duties to his teammates and would be content with passing and playmaking. Kevin Garnett came into the 2002-03 season hungrier and more intense than ever. He would still seek to facilitate for his teammates, but knew when to look for his shots. The hungrier Kevin Garnett would now take over games in tight situations instead of letting his teammates bail the team out. Not even injuries to high-scoring wingman Szczerbiak stopped Garnett from carrying the load of the team on his back. For the first time in his career, Garnett became a serious contender for the MVP award.

A hungrier and more focused Kevin Garnett would not stop piling up the stats. He would have his third triple-double of the season on December 27 when he had 25 points, 15 rebounds, and ten assists while winning in Chicago. And in the middle of January 2003, KG had his second 30-20 game of the season in a win against the Portland Trailblazers. He had 31 points and 20 rebounds in that match.

Because Garnett was climbing the MVP ladders as the season progressed, he would win his first Most Valuable Player award, albeit in a different category. In the year when Tim Duncan and Kobe Bryant were in the prime of their athleticism while Shaquille O'Neal was still his dominant self, Kevin Garnett shined brighter than any other Western All-Star when he had 37 points, nine rebounds, and five steals in the 2003 All-Star Game to win MVP honors.

A few games after the midseason break, Kevin Garnett had another 30-20 game. In a win against the Golden State Warriors on February 16, KG posted 37 points and 22 rebounds together with six assists and five blocks. And though it was in a loss to the Sacramento Kings on March 5, Garnett had 27 points and 24 rebounds. Barely two weeks later, he had another triple-double of 17 points, 11 rebounds, and ten assists. On April 6, KG had his sixth and final triple-double of the season in a big win over the Portland Trailblazers. He had 16 points, 14 rebounds, and 12 assists.

By carrying the Timberwolves with his ferocity and intensity, they broke their franchise win record and reached a new high of 51 wins in that season. Kevin Garnett remained one of the frontrunners for the MVP award, and his numbers supported that bid. He reached new career highs in all facets, averaging 23 points, 13.4 boards, and six assists in 40 minutes of play. He and Larry Bird became the only players to average more than 20 points, ten rebounds, and five assists in four straight seasons. Despite his considerable numbers, he finished a close second to his rival Tim Duncan for the MVP award.

Kevin Garnett could not catch a break in the playoffs as he, again, faced a powerhouse team. This time, it was the three-time defending champions the Los Angeles Lakers team standing in the way of the T-Wolves. Led by the dominant Shaquille O'Neal and dynamic superstar guard Kobe Bryant, the Lakers trailed to the T-Wolves one game to two. People started to think it would be a huge upset for the Timberwolves, and rightfully so because KG was so dominant in those wins. He had 35 points, 20 rebounds, and seven assists in the Game 2 win before finishing Game 3 with 33 points and 13 rebounds.

But it was not to be as the Lakers rallied back to win three straight games to effectively end Garnett's postseason and added another first round exit to the Timberwolves. KG was still a statistical demon in those consecutive losses but was merely a one-man show just as he was in the past six seasons for the Wolves, who were struggling to get talent. Garnett averaged another dominant stat line of 27 points, 15.7 rebounds, and 5.2 assists in the playoffs.

MVP Season

After another disappointing season for the Timberwolves and Kevin Garnett, the Minnesota team's executives knew that the roster they had at the time could not pay dividends for the team in the form of post-season success. Garnett was a once-in-a-lifetime kind of player. He was the legitimate franchise player and was at the point of his career where he could do everything. He could score, rebound, make plays, defend, and lead both vocally and by example. But it became evident he could not carry the team deep into the playoffs, especially with the supporting cast he had as teammates. The Timberwolves wanted to exorcise their first round demons, and they pulled out all the stops just to do that. The roster needed an overhaul to be more competitive.

KG had talented players on his team, but they just could not live up to his expectations. Terrell Brandon was a good acquisition, but was severely undersized at barely 5'11". Furthermore, the skilled point guard was injury prone. Chauncey Billups was also an excellent player. Unlike Brandon, Billups had the size to compete with and overpower other point guards. But, for some reason, he just could not get over the hump. It was not until his Detroit days that he became a perennial All-Star.

The shooting wingman Wally Szczerbiak was supposed to be Kevin's best complement. He became an All-Star but he never really meshed well with Garnett. [xvi] Even Kevin McHale thought that they never had good chemistry either in the locker room or on the floor. Former teammate and current Minnesota head coach Sam Mitchell thought that the problem with Wally was that he could not defend well, and that was one of the reasons why Garnett never got along with him.

Before kicking off the 2003-04 NBA season, the T-Wolves acquired capable centers Ervin Johnson and Michael Olowokandi to take turns manning the middle. Their best acquisitions and biggest pieces came in the form of two talented veteran perimeter players. The Minnesota Timberwolves traded Joe Smith and Anthony Peeler for former NBA champion point guard Sam Cassell. They hoped that Cassell would provide the stability they needed at the point guard position that Terrell Brandon and Chauncey Billups could not give them.

For the next piece, they acquired high-volume scoring small forward and multiple-time All-Star Latrell Sprewell in a four-team trade that involved Minnesota's Terrell Brandon. Sprewell was a talented scorer, but had a series of off-court issues in his career. However, he was just as passionate and fiery as KG was. At that moment, it seemed like Kevin Garnett had teammates with the right combination of skill, experience, and hunger to help him carry the load for the Timberwolves.

Though he had better options to help him offensively, Kevin Garnett's production did not even take a dip. In fact, he was even better playing alongside two other volume scorers. KG opened the season with a 20-20 game. He had 25 points and 21 rebounds to go along with six assists and three blocks. Then, on November 29, he had another similar game, finishing with 28 points and 20 rebounds in a loss to the Dallas Mavericks. Two games later, Garnett defeated the Sacramento Kings by owning the stat sheet. He had 33 points, 25 rebounds, and six assists. Those 25 rebounds were, at that time, a franchise best.

Despite the usual stat-stuffing nights from Kevin Garnett, who had 16 double-doubles in his first 20 games, the Wolves still looked like just a slightly better version of their previous selves. Nevertheless, they would win 13 out of their first 20 games. It was not until December when Garnett and company showed some semblance of being championship contenders. In fact, KG once again found his name leading the crop of MVP candidates.

As the Minnesota Timberwolves continued to find their groove as a team, Kevin Garnett was his usual fantastic self. On December 18, he would post his first triple-double of the season when he recorded 35 points, ten rebounds, and ten assists in beating the Dallas Mavericks before rounding up a successful month wherein the Timberwolves were 10-3.

Entering the New Year, Kevin Garnett delivered 27 points, 22 rebounds, and seven assists in his second game of 2004 before proceeding to be just as successful as he was in December for the month of January. Before the month ended, he had another triple-double in a loss to the Warriors. Garnett had 20 points, 20 rebounds, and ten assists in that game, but then proceeded to continue what was to become a 19-game double-double streak. Shortly after the midseason break, he even had 22 points and 24 boards against the Kings.

Though Kevin Garnett always had MVP stats for the last seven seasons or so, what was a better proof that he was more deserving of the award that season was how he was leading the Timberwolves to what was their best season in franchise history. And while doing that, KG was also putting up his best numbers all season long as the then-27-year-old big man in the prime of his career was thriving in leading his teammates by doing everything he can on both ends of the court.

Whether it was on the scoring end or the defensive side of things, KG was making his team better. One case in point was when he shot 5 out of 20 from the floor in a win against the Memphis Grizzlies near the end of the season. Despite the tough shooting night, he still ended up contributing by grabbing 22 rebounds and blocking four shots on the other end. With that kind of energy and intensity on both ends, Garnett led the Timberwolves to a nine-game winning run to end the season.

In addition to KG's improved leadership and skills, the offseason moves also looked to have paid dividends for the Minnesota Timberwolves. They improved their team record to an all-time Minnesota high of 58 wins. That was enough to take them to the highest seed in the ultra-competitive Western Conference, and they edged out the San Antonio Spurs for the spot with consecutive wins at the tail end of the regular season.

Finally, they were able to secure home court advantage, not just in their dreaded first round, but up until the Western finals.

Throughout the regular season, KG played his usual fantastic way. It could very well be the best individual season he has ever had in his career. In that season alone, he broke ten regular season Minnesota records on his way to putting up norms of his career high 24.2 points, career high 13.9, career high 1.5 steals, career high 2.2 blocks, and a steady amount of 5 assists. He grabbed his first rebounding title that season as well as another All-Star appearance.

As a testament to his dedication to improving his game and team, he was named to the All-NBA First Team and was awarded his first and only Most Valuable Player award, edging out perennial contenders Tim Duncan, Shaquille O'Neal, and Kobe Bryant for the coveted accolade. He became the first, and up to that date, only Timberwolves player to win the MVP award.[xvii]

As good as he was that season, Garnett could not have achieved that much if it were not for his perimeter threat duo of Sam Cassell and Latrell Sprewell. Cassell, a former champion with the Houston Rockets, had arguably his best season as a professional player. He averaged nearly 20 points to go along with more than seven assists on his way to his first and only All-Star selection.

The controversial player and equally fiery small forward Latrell Sprewell also had a productive season averaging nearly 17 points as a third scoring option and as a complement to Kevin Garnett. On top of that, high scoring wingman Wally Szczerbiak was a force to be reckoned with as the first choice off the Minnesota bench. The combination of Garnett, Cassell, and Sprewell was the highest-scoring trio in the NBA in that season, and every team they faced were put on their heels defensively.

In the playoffs, the high-octane trio did not disappoint and continued to perform at their highest levels. They first faced an upstart Denver Nuggets team with the high- scoring rookie and future star Carmelo Anthony. But the youth of the Nuggets could not contend with the hunger that Garnett and company displayed. KG was ready to exorcise his first round demons.

In Game 1 of that series, Garnett immediately made it known that he meant business as he finished the win with 30 points and ten rebounds. He was arguably better in Game 2 when he led the victory with a remarkable stat line of 20 points, 22 rebounds, and ten assists.

KG and his Wolves quickly dispatched the Nuggets in five games, achieving four wins to one loss. Each member of the Minnesota trio led the team in scoring at least one time in each of their wins with Sam Cassell scoring 40 in the first game and Garnett averaging nearly 30 points the entire series. Finally, the curse of the first round had been broken. They were able to bring Minnesota out of the first round for the first time in the entire existence of the franchise. But Garnett and company were not content with a first round series win. They wanted to reach the Finals to win the NBA title.

Their second round opponents proved to be one of their toughest opponents in the playoffs as they faced a veteran-loaded team in the Sacramento Kings. The Kings were also led by their high-scoring trio in All-Stars Chris Webber and Peja Stojakovic to go along with sharpshooting point guard Mike Bibby. The T-Wolves were on cloud nine after their first round victory, but were quickly pulled down to earth by the Kings as the Wolves lost the first game at home.

Kevin and company quickly bounced back by winning the next two games, including a road victory in Sacramento to regain control of home court advantage. In Game 2, Garnett had 28 points, 11 rebounds, and six blocks. It was an identical performance in Game 3 when he finished with 30 points, 15 rebounds, three steals, and five blocks for the Minnesota Timberwolves.

However, the Kings sent counterpunch after counterpunch by winning two of the next three games to send the series to an all-or-nothing seventh game in Minnesota. Garnett's scoring in those two losses was clearly in check. However, he did have 23 points, 12 rebounds, and three blocks to lead his team to a 3-2 lead before losing Game 6. This was the first time Garnett had to play a seven-game series, and it was the opportune time to show his ability as a player and a leader.

The Timberwolves were finally able to dispatch the mighty Kings at home in Minnesota with KG scoring ten straight points in the fourth quarter and saving his season with a block in the dying seconds. What was more amazing was Garnett's series stat line. In seven games, he played more than 46 minutes per game while averaging 32 points, 21 rebounds, and five blocks. It was evident that Garnett was indeed deserving of the MVP award. More importantly, his performance indicated that he wanted the championship trophy more than he ever did in his life.

With wins in the first two rounds, Kevin Garnett now proved his doubters wrong. Not only was he an MVP award winner, but he was also able to bring his team deep into the playoffs by making the Western Conference Finals, the deepest the Minnesota Timberwolves were able to reach in franchise history even up until now. There was no doubt that KG was the best player in the league at that time and the best player ever to wear a Timberwolves jersey.

The playoff run for the Timberwolves got tougher and tougher after every round. They were now facing a huge roadblock in the form of the Los Angeles Lakers, who were the three-peat champions two seasons prior. On paper, the Lakers were the best team in the league since they had four future Hall of Fame players on their roster. They were led by the ever-dominant Shaquille O'Neal, the sublime Kobe Bryant, a former Defensive Player of the Year Gary Payton at the point, and one of the best power forwards in the history of the game in Karl Malone. KG and the T-Wolves had to pull out all the stops to at least stand a chance of making it into the NBA Finals. Adding more woes to the Timberwolves, their backcourt star Sam Cassell went down with a back injury. It was up to reserve Troy Hudson to play the point.

The task at front proved too much for Kevin Garnett. He was the NBA's best player, but he could only do so much against a bruising frontline of O'Neal and Malone. The dominant O'Neal toyed with every player that tried to put a body on him. Shaq was an unstoppable force in the paint, but so was Karl Malone, who turned back the clock to have another chance to win the elusive NBA title. Malone scored 17 points two times, even while being defended by KG. He also held his ground defensively against the versatile Kevin Garnett.

In the end, the Lakers dispatched the T-Wolves in six games. KG tried to remedy the situation of losing his best point guard by bearing the burdens of playmaking for the majority of the series. However, the Lakers proved too much for him and his team. A lot of people, including Flip Saunders and Glen Taylor, believe that they would have beaten the Lakers had it not been for injuries. But, as they say, injuries are part of the NBA game. The Minnesota Timberwolves' dream season was crushed, and Kevin Garnett was forced back to the drawing board.

The Slow Breakup, the Building Frustration

After his MVP season, the 27-year-old Kevin Garnett was poised to become a free agent. However, he would agree to a $100 million extension over the next five years to stay with the T-Wolves.[xviii] The 2003-04 season was supposed to mark the start of a series of successful playoff runs for the Minnesota Timberwolves. It should have been the beginning of a dynasty to be as indicated by their successful run in the past season.

But it was not to be. It turned out that the previous season was the peak of what the franchise could ever reach concerning team success. As we all know, when you are at the summit of the mountain, you either stay on top, or you descend. In the case of the T-Wolves, they tumbled down from the peak, and it was not a methodical tumble. The Timberwolves just suddenly saw a quick decline that season.

The way KG played at the start of the season did not indicate how bad the Wolves would fall from the last season. The reigning MVP was balling like he was defending his crown as the best player in the world. He began the season with 28 points, 20 rebounds, seven assists, and three blocks in the opening day win against the New York Knicks. Then, on November 16, he had his second 20-20 game when he had 25 points and 21 rebounds together with eight dimes in a win versus the Heat.

With how Garnett was piling up enormous numbers and with the 13-7 record the Timberwolves had during their first 20 games, the MVP seemed like he was on his way to another great season both on an individual level and from a team standpoint. Kevin Garnett had piled up 18 double-doubles in just his first 20 games, and his rebounding numbers looked impressive even from his standards as an excellent rebounder. In 13 of those 18 double-doubles, KG had at least 15 boards.

Kevin Garnett's mastery of collecting misses continued, and the Big Ticket would compile 19 consecutive double-doubles from December 10 all the way to January 17, 2005. In one of those games, he tied the franchise record for rebounds when he collected 25 boards in a loss to the Orlando Magic. Unfortunately for him and his team, KG could not lead the Wolves to a good record in those monstrous games. Minnesota was 7 out of 12 in those 19 games. They would continue to tumble even lower by losing six straight games in February.

With another great individual season, Garnett was selected to his eighth overall All-Star Game. And while the Wolves were not as dominant as they were the past season, their leader still managed to force them to a good winning record after the All-Star break to try and battle for a playoff position. Minnesota would win 17 of their final 11 games. Along the way, KG had his first and only triple-double of the season in a win against the Golden State Warriors. He had 21 points, 15 rebounds, and 11 assists in that game.

Garnett played his usual self in the 2004-05 season. He was still the do-it-all big player he had always been since the start of his NBA career. He had averages of 22 points per game, 13.5 rebounds (leading the league), and 5.7 assists (highest among big men). His numbers earned him second All-NBA team honors as well as his typical appearance in the First Team All-Defense.

As good as KG remained, the Timberwolves only managed to win 44 games, 14 less than what they had the previous season. Sam Cassell, just one year after his best season, struggled to stay healthy. This hampered the T-Wolves' effectiveness at the point guard position. Sprewell remained healthy, but he could not repeat the production he had the previous year. Flip Saunders also struggled to juggle minutes between Sprewell and Szczerbiak.

And though the T-Wolves won the majority of their games, they could not reach the playoffs with the record that they had. Oh, how the mighty have fallen. The once great Timberwolves team was quickly brought back down to earth. It was the first time since Garnett's second season that the team failed to make the playoffs. It was indeed the start of the tumble of the Wolves, who were at the peak of their form the past year.

The following offseason proved to be one of the toughest for the Minnesota franchise. During the 2004-05 season, the T-Wolves management offered a three-year, $21 million dollar extension to Sprewell. Latrell felt insulted by the offer and even went public with his frustration with the contract, claiming that such an amount could not feed his family. He alienated the front office even until the offseason. With no team willing to take up Sprewell's contract demands, he was forced to retire after the 2004-05 season.

On the other side, Sam Cassell struggled to stay healthy the previous season. With Sprewell gone and Cassell inconsistent, the team decided to break up their core and shipped the latter along with a conditional first-round pick to the Los Angeles Clippers in exchange for the less efficient point guard Marko Jaric. Once again, it was up to Kevin Garnett to pick up the broken pieces and lift the team out of limbo and oblivion.

Kevin Garnett would try to force his way to get his team back to its winning ways without any significant help. Though it was a far cry from his fantastic start the past season, KG was still putting up good numbers in all columns of the stat sheet in the early stages of the season. At one point, he even led the Wolves to a winning record at that juncture of the year. However, that was the best they would accomplish during the 2005-06 season.

There was never a reason to fault KG for the Wolves' bad season. Garnett was still a superstar at the peak of his form but without any talented players to pass the ball to or to trust to take on more of the offensive and defensive burdens for the team. On December 15, KG had his first 20-20 game of the season when he put up 24 points and 21 rebounds in a loss to the Spurs. He even had six assists and four blocks that night.

The same narrative of Kevin Garnett posting high numbers while his team was losing continued all season long. In what was then a personal best of 34 consecutive double-doubles for him, KG posted several great all-around performances for himself despite the fact that the Wolves were less than mediocre. He had his second 20-rebound game on February 11 when he piled up 21 boards together with 19 markers. And in a win versus the Warriors on March 5, Garnett had 23 points and 21 rebounds. Two days later, he had 15 points, 21 rebounds, five assists, four steals, and two blocks in a loss to the Houston Rockets. That loss was the start of what was to become a seven-game losing skid for the Wolves.

In the 2005-06 season, Kevin Garnett averaged nearly 22 points, 12.7 rebounds (leading the league), and four assists, enough to earn him third team honors in the All-NBA selection. He was once again one of the best individual superstars in the league at that time when he was still at the height of his skills and athleticism. All of his individual accolades, however, were not enough, and the team continued to plummet downhill.

The team struggled once again the following season. They only had enough in themselves to win 33 games the entire season.

Minnesota just did not have the right pieces to win enough to make the playoffs. Marco Jaric and Troy Hudson could not fill in the gap that Cassell left at the point guard spot. Szczerbiak returned to the starting role in place of Sprewell, but he just did not have the right chemistry with KG to make the necessary impact. In the middle of the season, Wally was shipped over along with Olowokandi and another conditional first-round pick to the Boston Celtics for Ricky Davis, Marcus Banks, and Mark Blount. It was obvious that the Timberwolves were in rebuilding mode.

The 2006-07 season was just as dreadful as the previous ones. The Timberwolves still struggled to make the team better. They had lost their conditional first-round draft pick to the Portland Trailblazers. The pick turned out to be eventual Rookie of the Year and multiple-time All-Star Brandon Roy, who immediately paid dividends for the Blazers. Had the Timberwolves kept him, they would have added a complementary piece for their franchise player.

Kevin Garnett had to contend with the fact that he had to team up with less-than-stellar NBA players. His best option was the controversial Ricky Davis, who was considered a wasted talent because of his off-court drama and hard-headedness. Other than Davis, KG had to make due with role players like Mark Blount,

Mike James, Randy Foye, and Marko Jaric. Life was difficult for Garnett as a lone star in Minnesota.

Kevin Garnett would pile up 22 double-doubles in just the first 25 games of his season. And in the same 25 games, he had 18 games of scoring at least 20 points. The Wolves had no other choice but to rely on his scoring prowess all season long because of the lack of several other capable scorers on the team. His best scoring output at that point was when he had 31 points together with 14 rebounds in a win over the Utah Jazz on December 8.

Garnett had a new season high on January 1 in his first game of the New Year. In that win against the Charlotte Hornets, Kevin Garnett had 32 points together with 14 rebounds. He shot 12 out of 18 from the field in that game. He would then score at least 20 points in the next three games while piling up good rebounding numbers to lead the Wolves to a four-game winning streak.

In another win on January 13, Garnett tied a season high by putting up 32 points on 10 out of 19 shooting from the field against the New Jersey Nets. He also had 14 rebounds and four assists in that game. He would once again score that many points when the Wolves came to Los Angeles in a game against the Clippers. In that win, KG shot 10 out of 19 while also compiling seven big steals.

Two days after that win against the Clippers, Kevin Garnett showed that he was still as good a scorer as anyone when he needed to be. In a win against the high-scoring Phoenix Suns, Garnett shot 18 out of 29 from the floor and 8 out of 10 from the free throw line to score a season high of 44 points. Garnett also piled up 11 rebounds and three steals in that game.

On February 7, Kevin Garnett had his first triple-double of the season, compiling 17 points, 15 rebounds, and ten assists in only 31 minutes in a blowout win against the Warriors. Four days later, he did it again by recording 26 points, 11 rebounds, and ten assists against the Boston Celtics. Against the very same team nearly a month later, Garnett had 33 points, 13 rebounds, and ten assists. Such performances proved that Garnett deserved another appearance in the All-Star Game.

Despite the fact that Kevin Garnett was as good of a player as anyone in the league, the Timberwolves still stumbled and were far from playoff contention. They would win less than 10 of their final games after the midseason break. In those games, KG even had two 20-rebound games. He had 22 boards with only 10 points in a loss to the SuperSonics on March 23. And on March 30, Garnett had 22 points and 20 rebounds in another loss to the

Heat. His final game for the season (and for the Wolves in his first stint with the team) was on April 9 when he had 17 points, ten rebounds, and six assists.

In what turned out to be his final season in his first go-around with the Minnesota Timberwolves, Kevin Garnett averaged 22.4 points, 4.1 assists, and led the league in rebounds for the fourth straight year with 12.8. He made the All-NBA Third Team, but it was evident he was no longer happy with the team's present state. At the age of 31, he was going past his prime already. His window to chase a championship was already closing, especially since the Timberwolves were now a rebuilding team. He could no longer be the centerpiece of a rebuilding franchise, especially with his age. On the other side, the Timberwolves front office seemed to have accepted the fact that they might have to trade the man they molded since 1995 from being a kid to a force to be reckoned with.

The Trade to the Celtics

Before trading Kevin Garnett, Glen Taylor spoke to him about Minnesota's state of affairs. Taylor wanted to do all that he could to help Garnett win and get to the promised land of NBA champions. However, the catch was that he knew what everyone else in the league knew—that it would take a long while for him to get KG some help for a chance at a title. But

Kevin told Taylor that he wanted to win and that he could help Minnesota to start winning again.

According to McHale, financial restrictions were the deciding factors in dealing KG out of Minnesota. Kevin Garnett, according to McHale, wanted a certain amount. Glen Taylor, however, wanted to be fair with the cap space that the team had. He wanted to sign everybody to a fair amount despite the fact that he had a superstar that could demand a larger sum than anyone else in the league. The financial restrictions, as well as the fact that the Wolves were going nowhere with the team that they had, were deciding factors to why Garnett had to be shipped elsewhere.

Several teams were interested in acquiring the versatile big man. The Los Angeles Lakers head coach at that time, Phil Jackson, wanted to make a move for KG. They would have wanted to pair him up with dominant scorer Kobe Bryant. A duo of Garnett and Bryant would have been the hardest working and most basketball-obsessed duo the league has ever seen. The Lakers wanted to make the push considering that Bryant had also threatened to sign elsewhere given the fact that he had no help in LA.

With that, the Lakers were frontrunners to the Garnett sweepstakes. LA offered Glen Taylor a package that included veteran versatile forward Lamar Odom along with a young center Andrew Bynum. Lamar Odom was as good and versatile as any other big forward in the league. However, he was inconsistent and often displayed questionable behavior. Meanwhile, Bynum, despite the promise that he was showing, was largely unproven. Glen Taylor wanted Bynum, but was unsure about Odom. Phil Jackson even thought that Taylor was on his way to LA to finalize a deal. However, it did not push through.[xix]

According to Garnett's agent Andy Miller, Cleveland also wanted to push for Garnett to pair him up with the up and coming LeBron James. However, the third team involved was not so sure about the move. In the end, it came down to either the Lakers or Boston Celtics whose package included an accomplished center in Al Jefferson. It would turn out that the two legendary rivals would not only duke it out on the hardcourt but also in trade wars.[xx]

In the end, the Minnesota Timberwolves dealt their prized big man to the Boston Celtics in a trade that included Al Jefferson, Ryan Gomes, Sebastian Telfair, Theo Ratliff, and Gerald Green. Miller thought that Taylor was deeply interested in what Jefferson had to offer as a big man to build on. And while many thought the Lakers had a better package, it was ultimately Glen

Taylor who decided for the Celtics because they did not want KG playing for a Western team. He did not want his team to play against Garnett four times a year, and possibly in the playoffs.

Glen Taylor remembered how Kevin Garnett was first against the trade. KG kept telling the owner that he wanted to stay in Minnesota and that he loved the franchise, the people, and the organization despite the obvious flaws, struggles, and hardships he had gone through with the team. He was their franchise player and the best player to ever wear a Timberwolves uniform.

Taylor would also remember that Garnett could have vetoed the trade or could have forced his hand at canceling it. However, when the Celtics also made the move to get hot shooter Ray Allen from the Seattle SuperSonics, it was evident that Boston was the place to be and the team to win a championship with. The prospect of playing with Paul Pierce and Ray Allen, who were both premier players in their respective positions, was all too convincing for Garnett. To this day, Taylor still has reservations about whether Garnett wanted to leave the team. In the end, he made the decision for his big man, and it was time to bid him farewell, for now.[xxi]

The New Boston Big Three

Kevin Garnett immediately signed a three-year $60 million deal for the Celtics.[xxii] He came into the Celtic training camp optimistic about their chances of getting deep into the playoffs and possibly winning an NBA title. They had a solid core of veteran future Hall of Famers in Kevin Garnett, high scoring wingman Paul Pierce, and three-point shooting king Ray Allen. All three players were multiple-time All-Stars and had a lot of individual accolades. However, they were all missing an NBA title. Thus, they played to their strengths and complemented the play of the other stars.

Kevin Garnett would anchor the inside defense and provide the necessary post scoring. Ray Allen would provide the outside shooting from kick out passes. And Paul Pierce would be the all-around scoring punch they would need when plays got broken down. They were then known as the modern era Boston Big Three and were the first All-Star trio that Boston would have since Larry Bird, Kevin McHale, and Robert Parish were in town.

Aside from his fellow Big Three members, Kevin Garnett also had help from several teammates all around the roster. Manning the point was a young Rajon Rondo, who had a lot of potential at the first guard position. They also had a lot of interior toughness in the form of Kendrick Perkins, who was a strong defender and rebounder. Tony Allen and James Posey provided tough perimeter defense as backups for Ray Allen and Paul Pierce respectively.

KG also reunited with his former Minnesota teammate Sam Cassell, who provided a veteran presence for the younger guards. Other veterans included big man PJ Brown and outside gunner Eddie House. On paper, this team was built to win. The only thing they had left to do was to prove they were also winners on the hardwood floor.

Doc Rivers, the Celtics head coach that time, said that the first thing Kevin Garnett asked of his teammates was to sacrifice themselves and their individual desires for the greater glory of an NBA title. From day one, KG was not in the mood to fool around. Even when wearing a different uniform, he was just as intense as he ever was.

Another indication of how Garnett was so fired up and intense on his quest for a title was when Doc Rivers and Ray Allen tried to try and get KG to calm his intensity down. It was in an exhibition game in Europe, and the Celtics were playing with the Raptors. Sam Mitchell was coaching the Raptors that year. He would say that Rivers and Allen talked to him to try and convince Kevin Garnett to calm down because they thought that the Big Ticket was just trying to impress everyone. But Mitchell, who used to be Garnett's teammate in Minnesota, told them that the big man was always like that every single day. Kevin Garnett's fist bumps to the chest and head banging found its way to Boston.

Celtics general manager Danny Ainge said that Garnett not only provided veteran leadership for the team, but also provided the much-needed intensity, enthusiasm, and toughness as the catalysts in changing the culture of the entire Celtics franchise. He was tough on everybody and even made teammate Glen Davis cry on a televised game. He was not soft during practices either and also scolded Brian Scalabrine and Leon Power during practice for cracking jokes.[xxiii]

With 'sacrifice' as one of KG's mantras coming into the 2007-08 NBA season, he embodied this idea from the first game up until the final buzzer of their last game. It was oh so clear that Kevin Garnett truly sacrificed for the sake of the team as his numbers took a dip. Nevertheless, he was still an all-around dominant force from both ends of the court as shown by his monstrous early performances.

In his first official game as a Celtic, Kevin Garnett immediately made known he meant business. In a 20-point win over the Washington Wizards, KG had 22 points, 20 rebounds, five assists, three steals, and three blocks. He then proceeded to put up at least 18 points, 13 rebounds, and five assists in his next four games as a Celtic before eventually leading Boston to an undefeated 8-0 record at the start of the season.

As the season progressed and the Celtics won more games, Kevin Garnett realized that he did not have to do everything to push his team to wins. Everyone was doing their share of carrying the load for Boston. Pierce was scoring very well, and Allen was spreading the floor and hitting big shots. The veterans did their part in policing the younger guys. Because of that, KG mellowed down his numbers and made sure he stayed true to the word "sacrifice." There were two instances wherein he did not even score in double digits while his team won games against the Knicks and the Cavs. The Celtics would win 20 of their first 22 games.

The man that led the league in rebounding the last four years clearly did not care about his numbers as the Celtics won game after game on their way to a historic season. Kevin Garnett, who was so used to piling up double-doubles and big rebounding numbers, focused on defense, leadership, and on keeping his team motivated as his numbers saw a dip for the betterment of the team. However, he did still have great performances that were reminiscent of the one-man show he put on in Minnesota.

An instance of one of Garnett's best all-around performances was when he had 21 points, 12 rebounds, five assists, and three blocks against an improving center in Dwight Howard and the Orlando Magic in a win on December 23. Then, on December 30 in the Celtics' final game of 2007, Garnett faced the Lakers for a rivalry game between the league's most storied franchises. In that win, he had 22 points, 12 rebounds, six assists, two steals, and three blocks in a classic KG stat sheet.

Despite the fact that Kevin Garnett was so used to piling up triple-doubles every season, he would not have one in that campaign, but on many occasions, came close to one. One instance was on January 21, 2008, in a win against the New York Knicks. Garnett had 20 points, 13 rebounds, and seven assists. Though he was accustomed to being a secondary playmaker for the team at the power forward spot, Kevin Garnett sacrificed that role in Boston to make sure that the team was playing the way they had to play to win. Nevertheless, KG was still as good of a passer as any other big man in the league and made things easier for his teammates.

As the dust settled, the Boston Celtics were surprisingly dominant after putting up nine straight wins twice in one season. They finished the regular season with a winning record of 66 wins, which topped the whole league. Still an All-Star, Kevin's numbers went down to barely 19 points, 9.2 rebounds, and 3.4 assists, but it made the team better. He was more of a defender rather than a scorer. He solidified the Boston interior and mentored Kendrick Perkins to be just as tough as himself defensively. He would also sometimes act as the team's facilitator. Danny Ainge would sometimes ask him to score more, but facilitating was just something Kevin Garnett could not get out of his DNA. Indeed, he personified sacrifice and unity on the floor. Doc Rivers would even call him a "superstar role player" for his unwavering sacrifice to make the team better.[xxiv]

Along the way to helping the Boston Celtics to a historic season, KG was not short of a few milestone moments. On March 8, 2008, Kevin Garnett surpassed the 20,000 career-point mark in a game against the Memphis Grizzlies. Garnett would headline the Eastern Conference All-Star team as the league's highest vote getter. Despite the fact that he was in a different uniform, Garnett's intensity and love for the game ignited his fans to stay true in their support for him.

Ray Allen and Paul Pierce were also selected to play in the midseason classic. Allen finished the season tallying 17.4 points on 39% shooting from behind the three-point line. Pierce led the Celtics in scoring with 19.6 points to go along with five rebounds and 4.5 assists. Kevin was no longer a lone All-Star on a struggling team. He was a complementary star playing with two stars that also complemented him.

Kevin Garnett also won Defensive Player of the Year, which was highlighted by a game-saving dive for the ball in the dying seconds of a playoff game. The award was a testament for a player who did nothing but defend the basket ever since he first stepped on an NBA court. Though the personal numbers did not show it, the Celtics' suffocating defense was proof of how Garnett manned the paint. He communicated with everyone on the defensive end to make sure there was no open spots or weak areas on the floor. He made everyone fight for loose balls and buckled down on the defensive end. Garnett fought for possessions and even banged with the biggest and strongest players inside the paint while never forgetting to cover the basket. All his passion for the game was fuel for the great defensive showcase he put on all season long.

Garnett was also the first ever Celtic to claim the award on a team whose history is filled with terrific defenders. On top of that, he was also third in MVP votes behind eventual MVP winner Kobe Bryant and rising star point guard Chris Paul. While the 2003-04 season was arguably Kevin's best season as an individual, the 2007-08 season would be his best as a team player. In just his first year with the team and despite the fact that he was playing with two other stars, there was no arguing that Garnett had become the leader and the beating heart of the Celtics franchise.

The Road to Becoming an NBA Champion

Having home court advantage throughout the playoffs proved to be a deciding advantage for Kevin Garnett and the Celtics. The quest for an NBA title began against a tough Atlanta Hawks team that looked to have been out of the bout in the first two games given that they lost big time in those two losses. Kevin Garnett had double-double outputs in those two wins.

Despite an excellent output from KG in Game 3, he could not force the Celtics to take a 3-0 lead as the Hawks fought hard to come within a point. Atlanta would tie the series up with another win in Game 4. The Atlanta Hawks pushed them to their limit and had to rout them at their home court in a deciding seventh game. After a tough series win against the Hawks, people began to again question Garnett's ability to lead a team in the playoffs since he has always struggled to get past the opening round.

Next up was a rising Cleveland Cavaliers team led by the all-around player and the man who would soon become the league's best player, LeBron James. LeBron pushed the Celtic

Big Three to their limit. He was a one-man wrecking crew going up against three future Hall of Fame players. But KG proved to be the deciding force in Game 1 when he led the Celtics in scoring. He had 28 points and eight rebounds in that win. With his double-double of 13 points and 12 rebounds, the Celtics went on to win Game 2 and take a 2-0 advantage.

Just like what the Hawks did, the Cleveland Cavaliers fought back in their home court. Despite their experience, Garnett and his fellow All-Stars struggled to contain LeBron James in those two games as the Cavaliers tied the series by winning Games 3 and 4. But KG would not allow his team to give away the lead. In Game 5, he had 26 points and 16 rebounds to give the lead back to his team before the Cavs suddenly tied it again in Game 6.

But numbers, experience, and home court advantage decided the outcome for Kevin Garnett and the Celtics. They dispatched LeBron James and the Cavaliers in another seventh game. With Paul Pierce and LeBron James duking it out in a shootout, Garnett's defensive intensity and presence on the floor was the driving force for that Celtics win. After winning the series, the Celtics were once again questioned about their ability to win in the playoffs.

In the Eastern Conference Finals, they were matched up with the Detroit Pistons. The Pistons were also a team loaded with veteran players and multiple-time All-Stars. Chauncey Billups led the team together with scorers Rasheed Wallace and Rip Hamilton. Defensive toughness was the Pistons' key in winning as several capable shot blockers manned the paint while Tayshaun Prince shadowed the perimeter. This was a team that won an NBA title and had been to the NBA Finals twice in the past five years. It was not going to be an easy task for KG and his Celts.

Kevin Garnett was aggressive on the offensive end as soon as the series started. He outmuscled and outgunned every defender that tried to place themselves on him. It was clear that he wanted to reach the NBA Finals—a feat he had never managed to do in the past. His aggressive scoring in the series helped the Celtics in dispatching the Detroit Pistons in six games.

At the end of the series, Garnett averaged more than 20 points per game. As soon as the final buzzer ended, Garnett and his Celtics were on cloud nine. After all, they were going to the NBA Finals. That was the first time not only for Garnett but also for his fellow Big Three members. It was also the first time for the Celtics as a franchise since 1987. But Garnett and company knew that celebrations would have to wait. They still had one more job to do—win the NBA title.

Rivalries were renewed in the 2008 NBA Finals. The Boston Celtics would face longtime rivals in the Los Angeles Lakers. These two teams have had a long history of battles in the NBA Finals dating back to the 60's and 80's. Moreover, the Celtics and Lakers were also the two teams with the most NBA titles. Incidentally, the last time the Celtics were in the Finals was back in 1987 when they lost to the Lakers. It would have been sweet revenge for the Celtics to win their 17th championship against the team that beat them in their last title run.

The Los Angeles Lakers were no doubt one of the best teams in the NBA that year. Three-time champion and MVP Kobe Bryant, who was at that time considered to be the best player on the planet, headlined the Lakers squad. He also had a lot of help. They had acquired big man Pau Gasol in a midseason trade. Gasol played the role of sidekick to Kobe, and he played it well. They were not short on role players either with veteran point guard Derek Fisher running plays and versatile forward Lamar Odom on the frontline together with Gasol. To top things off, nine-time NBA champion coach Phil Jackson coached the Lakers. If the Celtics were to end their 22-year title drought, this was the best time and against the best team to do so.

Kevin Garnett, Paul Pierce, and Ray Allen were aggressive from the opening tip. Garnett dominated and pushed around Pau Gasol on offense despite the fact that they did not differ much in size. It was KG's toughness and grit that had Gasol struggling to contain him. He also controlled the board the entire series, averaging 13 points per game.

Pierce was also scoring while Allen shot the lights out from three-point range. The trio could not do it on their own against Kobe Bryant and his Lakers. Their veteran players stepped up. Eddie House had terrific shooting games while PJ Brown turned the clock with a renewed vigor on offense. James Posey also made life tough for Kobe to score. Finally, after numerous years of playing alongside mediocre teammates and doing everything for the team, Garnett had the supporting cast that would help him achieve his dream of an NBA championship.

The Boston Celtics won three of the first four games, and in a memorable sixth game in Boston, they blew the Lakers out of the building to secure the fourth win of the series and their 17th franchise NBA title. Garnett scored 26 points and had 14 rebounds in the title-clinching game. He was solid all around, both offensively and defensively. Garnett averaged a double-double in all six games despite the fact that he often struggled shooting from the field. But it was evidently not a one-man victory as Pierce won Finals MVP.

As Paul Pierce recounted, he saw that Garnett immediately knelt on the floor crying tears of jubilation. This was a fiery man on the basketball court. He was so intense and strong. But at that moment, he just broke down, unable to believe that he had reached the pinnacle of success. The mere image of Kevin Garnett breaking down after that victory proved his passion and love for the game of basketball. "Anything is possible," he screamed during the post-game interview. Indeed, everything *was* possible because he was now an NBA champion after years of toiling and suffering through losing seasons and mediocre years.

Injury, Missed Title Defense

The following season, Kevin Garnett found himself in a position he had never experienced in the past—he was a defending champion. At the same time, the Celtics franchise had not experienced being defending champions since the 1986-87 season. The defending champions were just as hungry as they were when they were chasing the NBA title. Throughout the regular season, it seemed as if they did not want to cede the championship to anyone just yet. Of course, it was Kevin Garnett who had the biggest hand in keeping the Celtics hungry.

They started the season at an NBA history best of 27 wins and only two losses. The season included a 19-game winning streak. In the middle of that great and historic franchise start for the Boston Celtics, Kevin Garnett was not short of any fantastic performances and outputs. More content with sharing possessions and shot attempts, KG was not the big scorer he used to be. However, he did have good scoring outputs. One case in point was on November 12, 2008, when he had 25 points together with 12 rebounds in a win over the Atlanta Hawks. Garnett shot 10 out of 16 from the field in that game. Then, on November 26, he had 21 points, 13 rebounds, and four blocks against the Golden State Warriors before having 26 points, 14 rebounds, and four blocks on December 3 when they beat the Indiana Pacers by 18. Garnett only played 31 minutes in that game while shooting 11 out of 14.

Four days after beating the Pacers, the Boston Celtics did it again. This time, Kevin Garnett was all over the floor, just like the old times in Minnesota. He had 17 points, 20 rebounds, four assists, five steals, and a block in that win. In his next game, KG was more content with passing and facilitating in the Celtics' 34-point win over the Washington Wizards. He had 11 points, 12 rebounds, and seven assists in that game.

After the 19-game winning streak had been broken, Garnett's minutes dwindled down as Doc Rivers found it necessary to rest his star players to keep them fresh and healthy for the playoffs. Despite the decreased playing time, KG still had good performances in his right. In only 22 minutes of action in a 45-point beatdown against the Sacramento Kings on December 28, he had 21 points and 11 rebounds while shooting 10 out of 11 from the field.

Another similar performance in about the same amount of time was when he played only 24 minutes but contributed 20 points and nine rebounds in a 32-point win against the New Jersey Nets on January 14. Three days later, he had 12 points, ten rebounds, and six assists in only 27 minutes of action in a win over the Nets. Because of performances like those, Garnett and his Celtics had a seven-game streak of winning by double digits. It was looking as if the defending champions were more dominant than they were a season ago.

Garnett kept racking up career milestones as the 2008-09 season went by. He became the youngest player to reach 1,000 career games at the age of 32 years and 165 days. He was also named an All-Star for a 12th straight year, which is 3rd all-time most consecutive All-Star appearances. However, he injured his knee in a game against the Utah Jazz following the All-Star break.

After evaluation, the Celtics decided to shut their star big man out for the last 25 games of the season. He would average 15.8 points, 8.5 rebounds, and 2.5 assists. That was his lowest per game average for points and assists since his rookie season.

With KG gone, the Celtics limped in every playoff series. They came in as the second seed of the Eastern Conference but were heavily pushed into a seventh and deciding game against the seventh-seeded Chicago Bulls. Although the Celtics won the series, they bled for every win with four of the seven games going into overtime. It was evident that they sorely missed Garnett.

The Celtics ran out of gas in the second round after the heavily fought opening round against the Bulls. The eventual Easter Conference champions Orlando Magic led by rising big man Dwight Howard knocked them out in seven games after the Celtics led the series three wins to two. Howard dominated the paint and pushed his weight around against his defenders. Had Garnett been there, it could have been a different story. Paul Pierce believed that they would have won at least seven games and would have repeated as champions if it were not for KG's injuries.[xxv] Their longtime rivals the Los Angeles Lakers eventually won the title that year.

Return to the Finals

Kevin Garnett returned healthy in the 2009-10 season. The Big Three were still intact, and the Celtics also added key veteran pieces in Rasheed Wallace and Marquis Daniels. Moreover, Kendrick Perkins was improving his game as an essential starter while Rajon Rondo was budding into an All-Star. Similar to their previous season, Garnett and company led the Celtics to a strong start with 23 wins to 5 losses. They started hungrily and were intent on going back to the NBA Finals.

Despite coming into the season healthy, Kevin Garnett's age and injury history along with the wear and tear that his body had suffered since 1995 began wearing him down. At the age of 33, he was past his prime and was only going to get slower and older. Because of that, KG would have to play then-career lows in minutes as he tried to contribute to the Celtic cause as their leader and enforcer.

Oddly enough, KG would only have six double-double outputs in those 28 games wherein the Celtics started 23-5. His highest rebounding production at that juncture was only 13 despite the fact that he was a four-time rebounding leader in the NBA. While age and injuries were reasons for his decline in that regard, Garnett's trust in his teammate's ability to collect misses was also a factor to his decreased rebounding rate.

Kevin Garnett's scoring output suddenly saw a decline as well. In his first 28 games, KG would only score a high of as much as 26 points. It was in a loss against the Phoenix Suns early on. Garnett would find himself scoring less than 20 points most of the time and would only score above that number five times during that good start for the Celtics. However, the important part was that the team was winning, with or without great outputs from any of their Big Three.

However, Doc Rivers ultimately played his key players fewer minutes in the regular season as a precautionary measure for their health. Although relatively healthy, Garnett still frequently felt pain in his previously injured knee. He averaged less than 30 minutes that season. It did not stop him though, and he was still selected as an All-Star. It was his 13th consecutive appearance and was, at that time, a record for all-time straight appearances. The Celtics had four All-Stars that year with the Big Three and rising star Rajon Rondo making his first appearance. At season's end, Garnett averaged 14.3 points and seven rebounds, both of which were career lows since his rookie season.

Although the Celtics started the season strong, they would lose 27 games after their 23-5 start. Many attributed the string of losses to Doc Rivers resting his starters and playing them fewer minutes. They struggled to get home-court advantage in the first round with a 50-win season, which was good enough for a Division title and the fourth seed in the Eastern Conference.

Many analysts wrote the Celtics off as too old and injured to make any serious dent or impact in the playoffs. But Garnett and company proved them wrong. Despite the fact that the Boston Celtics struggled to win games during the regular season because of the fewer minutes that the star players were playing, the long-term effects of the rest were much more important for them, especially in the playoffs.

They quickly dispatched the Miami Heat in five games with Kevin Garnett manning the paint and collecting boards. Playing less than 30 minutes during the regular season, KG looked like a younger man in the playoffs as he normed his usual big-minute outputs against the Miami Heat in the first round. He started off with 15 points and nine rebounds in Game 1 and with a rest in Game 2. Following the rest, Garnett combined for 48 points in the next three games to win the series 4-1. It would appear that resting the stars was a good move on the part of Rivers, and the Big Three looked invigorated in the playoffs and were hungry for another title run.

Up next was a second round meeting with back-to-back MVP LeBron James and the top-seeded Cleveland Cavaliers. With the

Lakers dominating the West, the whole world wanted to see LeBron squaring up with Kobe in the NBA Finals in a battle of arguably the two best basketball players in the world. On his part, LeBron was also dominating the East in the past two seasons as he was quickly becoming the world's best player. It would seem that such a battle was going to happen when the Cavs easily defeated the Celtics in their opening game. LeBron muscled his way through the Celtic defense, and many critics predicted it would be this way throughout the series.

But KG and the Celtics dug deep into their veteran experience. Garnett scored 18 points and collected ten rebounds in Game 2 in the Cavs' home court. They blew them out with a 104-86 victory. Fellow veteran big man Rasheed Wallace scored 17 points that game while the young point guard Rondo dished out 19 dimes. The Celtics lost home court advantage when the series went to Boston. The Cavs blew them out on their home floor, and they trailed two games to one. Nevertheless, Garnett still had 19 points in only 30 minutes of action in that match. It was a sign that the big man was not losing his touch, even in losses.

After making necessary adjustments, the Celtics won Game 4. Garnett had another decent output in that win as he finished with 18 points on 6 out of 11 shooting from the field. The series returned to Cleveland for Game 5, but the Celtics ran roughshod over the hapless Cavs to win in a blowout. Garnett had 18 points that game. It was in the midst of that game that the Celtics regained their form and where people began to question LeBron's will to win as he disappeared and quit on his team.

The series shifted to Boston for Game 6, and it was on their home court where they would finally dispatch the Cavs. Kevin Garnett led the way for the Celtics with 22 points and 12 rebounds. It seemed like KG turned the clock back during that series. As phenomenal as Garnett was, it was ultimately Rondo who controlled the series for the Celtics. He was instrumental in making plays for his veteran teammates and making life easier for the older Big Three. He even tallied a triple-double in Game 4. However, Kevin Garnett was still the vocal leader and inspirational figure that got the Celtics playing intense against the best team in the East.

Silencing their critics and breaking fans' dreams of a LeBron-Kobe Finals, the "old and slow" Celtics marched into Orlando to once again face Dwight Howard, the league's best big man, and the reigning Easter Conference champions Orlando Magic. This time, the Celtics had KG and more experienced help in the middle to handle the dominant Dwight Howard. Boston defeated the Orlando Magic on the latter's home court in the first two games.

In those two wins, Kevin Garnett did not score as much as he did against the Cavs since he focused on helping out defensively against the dominant Dwight Howard. KG combined for only 18 points, but had 20 rebounds in Games 1 and 2. But because the two wins were close, people began to speculate that the whole series would be equally as tight. However, the Celtics would win against the Magic in blowout fashion back in Boston to establish an insurmountable 3-0 lead. Garnett would even only play 23 minutes in that game.

No team in the history of the NBA has ever come back from a 3-0 deficit in the playoffs to win the series. People began to write the Magic off, but Orlando would not make things easy for KG and company. They would win the next two games and staggered the Celtics. In the sixth game of the series, the most unlikely of heroes saved the Celtics from a devastating seventh game in Orlando. Undersized backup point guard Nate Robinson took over for the injured Rajon Rondo and hit two clutch long-range shots to seal the series for the Boston Celtics. The Celtics had paved a tough road on the way to a return to the NBA Finals. Meanwhile, familiar foes were paving their return to the Finals.

History has always loved pitting the two most successful NBA franchises against each other in the NBA Finals. It was the 12th time in NBA history that these two teams had met. In one corner, the battered Celtics were an older team filled with veterans. The usual Big Three together with star point guard Rajon Rondo led them on their way to a Finals berth. In the other corner, the Los Angeles Lakers remained kings of the West. They had just won an NBA title the previous year and were on their way to a third consecutive trip to the NBA Finals. They held their core intact with Kobe Bryant and Derek Fisher in the backcourt together with offseason acquisition Ron Artest manning the perimeter. While Kobe Bryant remained a dominant superstar, it was the Lakers frontline that would prove to be more devastating. Seven-footer Paul Gasol and a young rising star center Andrew Bynum anchored the paint while versatile power forward Lamar Odom was coming off the bench. The Celtics frontline, manned by Garnett, would have to dig deep to push the trio of big men back.

The Celtics would lose the opening game at Los Angeles by 12 points. They could not stop Kobe Bryant from scoring, and the Laker frontcourt devastated them on the boards. Things would take a turn to the Celtics' favor as Ray Allen found his groove in the second game. He hit a Finals record of seven three-pointers in one game while Rajon Rondo filled the stats sheet with a triple-double to tie the series 1-1. Kevin Garnett would wake up from a slumber in game three as he hit the Lakers with 25 points. However, the Lakers would regain home court advantage that game, and Kobe once again scored at will while the Lakers' twin behemoths secured the rebounds.

With their backs up against the wall at a 2-1 deficit, the Celtics would turn to their bench in the fourth game. Glen "Big Baby" Davis led the way for the bench with 18 points while reserve point guard Nate Robinson added 12. The Celtic bench doubled the Laker bench's production. In game five, the Celtics would return to their starters for production. Paul Pierce led the way with 27 points including a game-clinching save to Rondo. Kevin Garnett returned to form with 18 points and a team-high ten rebounds. Rondo was also spectacular with 18 points and eight assists. The Celtics controlled the series with an advantage of three wins to two. They were now only one win away from hoisting their 18th championship banner.

With the Lakers trailing, head coach Phil Jackson remained calm heading into Boston for game six, claiming that the 3-2 deficit was still basically the result of home court advantage. While the Lakers had their usual stars producing decent numbers for them, it was their bench that did the Celtics in.

They blew the Celtics out 89 to 67. The worst part for Boston was that their starting center Kendrick Perkins was diagnosed with a serious knee injury that kept him out of the defining game seven. The Celtics would now have to rely on old faithful Kevin Garnett and backup Rasheed Wallace to hold back the Laker frontline.

The Celtics' worst nightmares came true. They were in dire need of Perkins' rebounding and defending as the Laker frontline devastated them inside and on the boards. As good as Garnett was, he could not handle an imposing frontline on his own especially with Wallace fouling out. The Boston Celtics kept fighting back and even held a big lead, but the Laker veterans Derek Fisher and Ron Artest hit clutch basket after clutch basket to mount a comeback. In the end, the Lakers proved too much for KG and his Celtics. Kobe Bryant and his Lakers hoisted the trophy to the dismay of the Celtic leader in what would be his final trip to the NBA Finals to date.

Battling Against the Newest Big Three

After a disappointing loss in the NBA Finals, the Celtics added big pieces to their frontline to spell the injured Kendrick Perkins and to prevent opposing centers from imposing their will on the depleted Celtics. They acquired one of the best centers in NBA history, Shaquille O'Neal, and former All-Star Jermaine O'Neal, both of whom were on the tail ends of their respective careers. Garnett would remain healthy for the start of the 2010-11 season and led the Celtics once again to a good start with a record of 23 wins to only three losses.

KG would again have great performances as the Celtics were trying to reclaim their hold over the Eastern Conference where a power surge had abruptly happened during the offseason. One of Garnett's best games at the start of the campaign was when he had 24 points and ten rebounds in only 29 minutes to beat the New York Knicks early on. After that, he had 22 points in their next game, which was against the Detroit Pistons. Then, on November 26, 2010, KG had 26 points and 11 assists to help his team win against the Toronto Raptors. A week later, he had 20 points, 17 rebounds, and six assists to beat the Chicago Bulls. From the way he started the season, it did not seem like Garnett was already 34 years of age.

Similar to how the Celtics slowed as the season went on, Kevin Garnett's performances began to wane as age and injuries caught up with him again. Arguably, his presence on the court was one of the biggest reasons why the Boston Celtics were able to get off to such a good start. Unfortunately for them, they would be missing the services of the Big Ticket for a while in the middle of the long campaign.

Much like what happened two years ago, Garnett would injure his right knee and would miss two weeks. It was during his absence when the Celtics struggled considering that their defensive frontline had depleted. Kevin Garnett would return from his two-week absence in a win over the Orlando Magic. He had 19 points and eight rebounds in that return game. Two games later on January 21, he had 21 points in only 25 minutes of action while making 7 of his ten field goal attempts. Another one of his better performances was on January 30 in a rematch game versus the Lakers. He had 18 points, 13 rebounds, and five assists in that win. Although they were met with a setback sometime in the middle of the season, KG made the All-Star team for the 14th time, once again increasing the record for most consecutive All-Star game selections.

Kevin Garnett began to look better just after the midseason break. In his first game back after the All-Star Weekend, he had 24 points, 12 rebounds, and six assists to beat the Warriors by 22. Then, on March 2, he had a season high of 28 points together with 11 rebounds in a win versus the Portland Trailblazers. KG would have four more games of scoring at least 20 points from then on until the end of the regular season. He also added four more double-double performances for himself.

At the end of the 2010-11 season, the veteran would average nearly 15 points and almost nine rebounds. Despite the fact that his numbers continued to look mediocre as he aged deeper into his 30's, Kevin Garnett looked better than most guys at his age. He was shooting a personal all-time high of 52.8% from the floor while continuing his mastery at the defensive end for his team. More importantly, his Celtics marched into the playoffs as the third seed.

The Celtics easily handled the New York Knicks in the opening round. They swept the Big Apple team in four games. Garnett did not have the best shooting performances in that series and focused on the rebounding and defending. He had double-digit rebounds all series long before closing the Knicks out with 26 points and ten rebounds in Game 4. After an easy opening round, things quickly took a turn for the worse for the Celtics as they met the revamped Miami Heat.

The Miami Heat were fresh off a historic offseason. They had acquired LeBron James and Chris Bosh via free agency while keeping Dwyane Wade on the roster to form their version of the Big Three. This new incarnation of a dominant trio was one of the legacies that Kevin Garnett left. When he and Allen moved over to Boston, other teams followed suit considering that the Celtic Big Three was nearly unbeatable. James, Bosh, and Wade could not beat them on their own, but as a trio, things were different.

The meeting between the two teams was a changing of the guard. The Celtics had an older yet more accomplished Big Three trying to hold their own against a younger and hungrier trio of Miami stars. In the end, youth triumphed over experience. The Miami Heat beat the Celtics in five games despite Garnett hitting a playoff high 28 points together with 18 rebounds in their lone victory in Game Three. Out with the old, and in with the new. It was not how the Celtics would have wanted their season to end. The Miami Heat simply had youth on their side while the Celtics were getting older and were getting weary with the mileage of their three main stars. Luckily for KG and the rest of the older fellows, they would have a lot of time to rest during the long offseason.

Not many NBA superstars can say they have experienced two lockouts in their career, but Kevin Garnett is one of the few. The NBA experienced another lockout in the 2011-12 season, and it was not until December that the league resumed activities and started a new season. The extra two months of off-time would have been helpful for the aging Boston Celtics to rest their bones, but the lack of a training camp kept them rusty to start the season.

It was also a transition period for the 35-year-old Kevin Garnett. With Kendrick Perkins traded to the OKC Thunder the previous season and with Shaquille O'Neal enjoying retirement, Garnett was forced to man the middle as the Boston Celtics' starting center, a position he was never fond of playing. Along with rust, it was one of the reasons as to why KG struggled at the start of the shortened campaign.

It would take until his seventh game of the season for Garnett to collect his first double-double in a win against the New Jersey Nets. In that match, he had 14 points and 12 rebounds. However, the Celtics would face a rare five-game skid after that win despite a few good performances for the aging Kevin Garnett in that losing streak.

The Celtics limped to a record of 15 wins to 17 losses by the All-Star break. It was the first time in the Big Three era that this had happened. Moreover, Kevin Garnett's All-Star selection streak was broken as he failed to produce All-Star worthy numbers. It was the first time since his sophomore season that the legendary Garnett failed to make the All-Star team. But like a car running on diesel, it would take time for the KG and his Celtics to get back into form.

After the snub, Garnett proved he was still All-Star material after posting 25 points and ten rebounds in a win over the

Milwaukee Bucks on February 29. He then followed that up with 20 points and ten boards to win against the Nets before beating the Knicks with his 18 markers and ten rebounds. While he was never about personal accolades, those performances showed that KG was probably annoyed by the fact that he was not selected as an All-Star.

Kevin Garnett would have a few more remarkable performances up his sleeves. On March 28, he had 23 points, ten rebounds, four assists, two steals, and a block to show what classic KG looked like back in Minnesota. In his very next game, he had 24 points, ten rebounds, and four assists while shooting 12 out of 18 in a blowout win versus his old team, the Timberwolves. Then, on April 10 in a hard-fought win against the Heat, he had 24 points and nine rebounds before turning in 22 points and 12 rebounds in a win against the Hawks in the very next day.

Like championship contenders do, KG and his Celtics found their groove as the season progressed. After starting the season 15-17, they proceeded to win 24 of their next 34 games to qualify for the playoffs as one of the higher-ranked teams in the East. They ended the season as the fourth seed with a 39-27 record. Garnett averaged almost 16 points and eight rebounds in the lockout-shortened season.

KG and the Celtics would face the Atlanta Hawks in the opening round of the playoffs. The younger Hawks were a tough matchup, but would soon fall in six games to the experienced Celtic squad. Boston would once again face a young team in the form of the Philadelphia 76ers. Similar to Atlanta, the young legs of the Sixers gave the older Celtics a run for their money and forced them to a seven-game series. At the end of the day, it was still the Celtics that came out triumphant.

The Celtics found themselves once again in the Eastern Conference Finals with another crack at making the NBA Finals. A familiar roadblock stood in their way. It was the Miami Heat, the previous year's finalists and the team that eliminated the Celtics in the last playoffs stood mighty and would also want another chance at the NBA Finals. It was once again a battle of the Celtic Big Three against their Miami Heat counterparts.

With Boston losing the first two games against Miami (though they sent Game 2 into overtime), people began to murmur that they were too old to contend for an NBA title and that they would once again easily fall to the searing hot Heat team. Kevin Garnett would have none of it. He scored a team high 24 points along with 11 rebounds to help the Celtics win Game 3. He was once again instrumental in the game four victory by pulling down 14 rebounds. With the series tied at 2-2, Garnett would lead the way for the Celtics by winning a close bout in Miami. He scored 26 points and 11 rebounds.

The Celtics were only one win away from reaching the NBA Finals for the third time in the Big Three era. But the reigning MVP LeBron James would impose his will on the Celtic defense by scoring 45 points while collecting 15 rebounds on a dominant and memorable performance that gave the Heat a blowout victory over the Celtics.

Boston tried to fight back in Game 7 on the Heat floor. Once again, LeBron was just too great of a player to cede the Eastern title to the Celtics. He finished the series-clinching win with 31 points and 12 rebounds to once again end the season for the Kevin Garnett and the Celtics. While KG was dubbed as too old to lead a team at that point of his career, he did find his younger self in the playoffs by averaging 19 points and 10 rebounds. But it was not enough to hand another title to the Celtics franchise. Since then, Kevin Garnett has yet to go farther into the playoffs.

The End of an Era and the Trade to Brooklyn

The Celtics needed to add younger talent to a rapidly aging roster. In the offseason of 2012, they drafted Jared Sullinger and Fab Melo to add some youth to the frontline. They re-signed wing scorer Jeff Green, who had missed the previous season due to a cardiovascular illness. Kevin Garnett also re-signed with the team, and the latter's contract was reported to be a three-year deal worth $36 million with a no-trade clause.[xxvi] KG contemplated retiring before re-signing with the team, but he felt like he had more gas in him to make a run at another title. But to Boston's dismay, Ray Allen signed with their nemesis the Miami Heat for a lot less money to have a better chance at another title run. That move marked the end of the modern-era Boston Big Three.

With Ray Allen gone, KG and Paul Pierce had to pick up the heavy load of scoring for the team. They lost the third head of their fearsome trio, but were banking on Rajon Rondo to be able to fill the void that Allen left. However, Rondo's season ended abruptly in January 2013 when he tore his ACL. With his star guard out, Garnett doubled up his efforts on the offensive end and was able to return to the All-Star team. That was his 15th, and to date, final All-Star game appearance.

At 36 years old, Kevin Garnett still had gas left in the tank to put on some good performances. Early in the season, he had 20 points and 13 rebounds in a win over the Washington Wizards. Later on against the Magic, he had 24 points and ten rebounds in a win for the Celtics. And while it would take a few more months for him to crack 20 points again, he did on January 27, 2013, against the Miami Heat. He had 24 points, 11 rebounds, four assists, two steals, and three blocks in that game. Then, on February 10, he pulled down a season high of 18 rebounds in an overtime win against the Denver Nuggets. He also had 20 points, six assists, two steals, and three blocks in that classic performance for the elder statesman.

In that season, KG also reached the 25,000 career point mark against no less than their longtime rivals the Los Angeles Lakers. At the end of the season, KG averaged nearly 15 points and almost eight rebounds while playing less than 30 minutes per game. The Celtics would win 41 games, their lowest since 2004, but it was still a good enough performance to make it to the playoffs where they were beaten by the Carmelo Anthony's New York Knicks in six games. That would be the last playoff series Kevin Garnett would be playing in as a Celtic.

Realizing that they were no longer the powerhouse squad that they were when the Big Three got together in 2008, Celtics management decided to start fresh in the 2013-14 season by dismantling the roster. They started off by getting rid of the massive contracts of Kevin Garnett and Paul Pierce, both of whom served the team wholeheartedly.

KG and Pierce (together with Jason Terry) were traded to the Brooklyn Nets for first round draft picks in 2014, 2016, and 2018. The Celtics also received a handful of players (Kris

Humphries, Keith Bogans, Kris Joseph, Gerald Wallace, and MarShon Brooks) in exchange for the two future hall of fame players. Respecting the team's decision in trying to rebuild for a brighter future, Kevin Garnett waived his no-trade clause. The trade officially ended KG and Pierce's run in Boston where they first got a taste of what it felt being on top of the basketball world.

Brooklyn Stint

KG had ended a sweet 6-year partnership with the Boston Celtics. He was now bound for New York to suit up for the Brooklyn Nets. Unlike the Celtics, the Nets were trying to go deep into the playoffs and also gain popularity after having relocated to Brooklyn from New Jersey the previous year. In doing so, they assembled a starting five with a combined 35 All-Star appearances and a roster payroll total of over $100 million.[xxvii] Garnett and Pierce were set to join then star point guard Deron Williams, All-Star wingman Joe Johnson, and a young, but very talented center Brook Lopez. In addition to a star-studded starting squad, the Nets also hauled up their bench with talented players like former All-Star Andrei Kirilenko, Shaun Livingston, and athletic rookie center Mason Plumlee. This team was to be coached by former All-Star point guard Jason Kidd. With a stronger lineup, KG was confident that he would get another chance at a title run.

With all their title aspirations and money spent on strengthening the roster, the Brooklyn Nets struggled to make even a dent in the league. By the end of 2013, they had only managed ten wins. The conflict was attributed to multiple injuries to key players and rookie coach Jason Kidd's struggles in his new job together with his feud with assistant coach Lawrence Frank. Adding further trouble to the roster, the Nets lost star center Brook Lopez to a season-ending injury. As silly as it sounds, the injury to Lopez turned out to be a gift for the Nets.

The league was in a transition phase. No longer would you see two gigantic big men on the floor and in the paint at the same time. The league was going in a direction where most teams would play only one true big man in the paint and surround the perimeter with shooters. Jason Kidd used this to his advantage and started Kevin Garnett at center while moving Pierce and Johnson up from their usual positions. They would also start two point guards at the same time. The Nets now began to play a smaller roster, and it was to their benefit.

KG played his usual brand of tough interior defense while playing center. As the league began to play smaller and smaller, imposing and gigantic centers also began to disappear. While

Garnett always hated playing the center position, he could now do so without worrying about opposing centers dominating the paint. Garnett would also collect a career total of 14,000 rebounds joining an elite class of only ten players who have done so in their career. By reaching 14,000 rebounds, he also became the third player in league history to have 25,000 career points, 14,000 career rebounds, and 5,000 career assists. The only two players to have done so are Karl Malone and Kareem Abdul-Jabbar. Not too shabby of a company to be included with.

In his first and only complete season with the Nets, Garnett averaged career lows in points and rebounds with 6.5 points and 6.6 boards while mostly playing the role of interior defender. His point production was a surprisingly far cry from what he was producing in his final season in Boston. Nevertheless, the important part was that he was still winning games.

The newly rejuvenated Nets roster made a run from January up to the end of the regular season to secure a playoff spot as the sixth seed in the East. With the experience and smarts that their players had, they defeated the higher-placed Toronto Raptors in the first round of the playoffs in a pivotal seventh game. After winning the first round, KG would now once again face the dreaded Miami Heat trio that had tormented him several times in his career. This time, people were talking about an upset series win for the Brooklyn Nets since they were the only team to have swept the Heat in the regular season ever since they formed their own Big Three. The Nets were confident they could beat the Heat in a seven-game series, if not sweep them again.

However, the Nets' confidence was misplaced. The Miami Heat ran roughshod over the hapless Brooklyn Nets, beating them in five games. The Heat would beat the Nets by double digits in the first two games and then win games four and five in close outputs. LeBron James simply overpowered the Nets' defense by top scoring in all five games and with a 49-point output in the fourth match. Once again, LeBron James foiled Kevin Garnett's run at another NBA title. It would also be KG's final playoff series to date.

Minnesota Homecoming

Because the Nets still struggled to win games in the 2014-15 season after losing Pierce to free agency and while both Deron Williams and Joe Johnson struggled to get back to All-Star form, they decided to trade away Kevin Garnett to the Minnesota Timberwolves in exchange for Thaddeus Young. To give effect to the trade, the legendary forward once again waived his no-trade clause for an unprecedented third time to go home to the franchise that had drafted him and molded him into a Hall of Fame caliber player.[xxviii] KG would play 42 games for Brooklyn that season while averaging 6.8 points and 6.8 rebounds.

Minnesota would welcome their prodigal son with open arms in a game against the Wizards. Garnett's return to the Timberwolves brought new life to the crowd. As young forward Andrew Wiggins would recount, Minnesota was a ghost town. The Timberwolves rarely sold out their games before Garnett's return. But KG's presence on the team brought the people of Minnesota together and rejuvenated their love for the team.[xxix]

In his homecoming to Minnesota, Garnett was now an NBA champion, but at 38 years of age, he was coming to the tail end of his career. That season, he would only play five games for the franchise where he spent his first 12 years as a pro, averaging 7.6 points and 5.2 rebounds. With a rebuilding team centered on soon-to-be Rookie of the Year Andrew Wiggins, the T-Wolves would miss the playoffs and ended that season with the worst record in the NBA. It was also the first time since his first season in Boston that Kevin Garnett would miss the playoffs.

Kevin Garnett contemplated retiring at the end of the 2014-15 season. He was 38 years old and no longer the imminent threat he once was. He could no longer make a serious impact when placed on any team at that point in his career. However, the Timberwolves and head coach Flip Saunders convinced him to sign a two-year deal with the team. As Flip recounted, KG never wanted to leave Minnesota, even during his first run with the team. Garnett was finally home and was not going anywhere soon. [xxx]

The Minnesota Timberwolves' offseason started very well when they landed the first overall pick in the 2015 NBA Draft. As all the analysts predicted, the T-Wolves drafted the favored number one draft choice Karl-Anthony Towns from Kentucky. The 7-foot tall Towns would join a roster filled with young talent such as Ricky Rubio, Gorgui Dieng, Shabazz Muhammad, Slam Dunk champion Zach LaVine, and reigning Rookie of the Year Andrew Wiggins.

Tragically, before the season could even get started, the Timberwolves lost their president and head coach Flip Saunders to Hodgkin's lymphoma at the age of 60. No Timberwolf was more devastated by the loss of Flip than Kevin Garnett. Flip was the man who first believed in the 19-year old rookie and inserted him into the starting lineup. He was the one who gave confidence to "Da Kid" and helped him forge a legendary career.

Flip gave Garnett a chance to be a superstar by trusting him since his rookie year. KG's former coach did not see anything special in the rookie, but Flip did. He chose the 19-year-old KG over then veteran player Christian Laettner to start as the power forward spot and become the primary focus on offense. Above all, Saunders trusted KG to be the franchise player in Minnesota for over a decade. He had a lot of other options for talented players play for him in the Timberwolves, but still chose Garnett over and over again to be the man to build on. Flip had more than a thousand victories in his storied coaching career. Without KG, that number would have been significantly less. In turn, Garnett had over 25,000 points and 14,000 in a surefire Hall-of-Fame playing career. Without Flip, Kevin may not have flourished into a superstar of such a high caliber.

As a heartfelt tribute to a man who was like a father to him, KG went to the Timberwolves practice facility, sat in Flip's empty parking spot, and posted a photo of it on Facebook with the caption "Forever in my heart." The tribute was oddly very simple for Kevin Garnett, a man who talks a lot both on and off the floor. There were no long speeches or lengthy messages—just a single photo that meant so much. The simplicity of KG's message to his fallen "father" is testament showing that it was a personal, heartfelt message to the man who gave KG a chance to shine as a superstar.[xxxi]

The team went into the 2015-16 season with heavy hearts but with renewed vigor as a tribute to the man who was technically the father of their team. Sam Mitchell took over the team as the interim head coach. As far as Garnett's part, everyone in the team knew he would no longer dominate and take over games. The one main reason why Flip brought him back to Minnesota was to be a mentor to the younger players, especially for Wiggins and Towns.

KG would respect his fallen coach's wishes and would teach everything he knew about the game of basketball to his younger teammates. As he jokingly said about mentoring the young T-Wolves, "It's like putting puppies in a box, shaking it, and watching them go at it."[xxxii] With him playing a leadership role, the T-Wolves started the season strong and continued to exceed expectations.

Looking like a man content with the NBA life and career he had spent, Kevin Garnett never looked so happy to be on a losing team in his entire life. Everyone in the world knew that KG could no longer impact games the way he used to. That may have been true on the court, but off the court, he was a significant factor to his younger teammates' growth.

On November 15, 2015, Kevin Garnett became only the fifth player to have ever played 50,000 career minutes, joining the likes of Kareem Abdul-Jabbar, Jason Kidd, Elvin Hayes, and Karl Malone. He then moved up that list on December 1 to become third overall and by passing his former head coach Jason Kidd. Then, on December 5 in a loss to the Portland Trailblazers, Garnett scored 5 points and became one of the 15 players in league history to surpass 26,000 career points.

Then, on December 11, Kevin Garnett grabbed five rebounds in a loss to the Denver Nuggets and became the NBA's all-time leader in defensive rebounds. He would pass Karl Malone in that regard. That record speaks so much of KG's tenacity to secure and make sure he put an explanation point to his defensive stops. By racking up defensive rebounds in bunches in more than two decades, Garnett was the embodiment of what it was to truly complete a defensive play. Defense never stops until you grab the rebound.

However, Garnett would eventually miss more than half of the season because of an injury that has plagued him for nearly ten years. The same right knee injury that derailed his title defense during the 2008-09 season was the very reason as to why he had to get shut down on January 25, 2016, until the end of the season. But little did the world know that Kevin Garnett had played his final NBA game on January 23. He had 2 points in only 9 minutes of action in that match.

Retirement

Kevin Garnett spent most of the remaining time of the 2015-16 season and the following offseason to recuperate from his ailing injury in the hopes of making a comeback in the next season for the promising Minnesota Timberwolves. The content champion and MVP was witness to how his peers and contemporaries had retired their sneakers to go fishing for the rest of their lives perpetually.

The first of his contemporaries to announce retirement was Kobe Bryant, who had spent much of his final season on a farewell tour with the struggling Los Angeles Lakers. Unlike KG, Kobe went out smoking as he scored 60 points in his last NBA game. Then there was Tim Duncan, his old rival at the power forward position, who had announced retirement shortly after the season ended. Though Timmy, like Garnett, still had enough gas left in the tank, the wear and tear had slowed him down too much that he was not sure he could handle another 82-game grind.

With two of the other best players in his era deciding to hang their boots up for good, on September 23, 2016, Kevin Garnett announced that he would follow suit. After 21 years in the NBA,

Kevin Garnett was finally retiring. There were no flashing lights or farewell tours for KG. All he did was post a social media video of him thanking the world for the opportunity he got and to say goodbye, not just to basketball, but to the fans that had come to love his passion, intensity, and love for the game.

In retrospect, no other player in the league was ever like Kevin Garnett. His mouth was unmatched when it came to trash-talking and bad-mouthing opponents and teammates alike. His work ethic for the game was unlike any other. He brought intensity to every team he played for while never forgetting to be the vocal and emotional leader of the squad. For 21 years, KG did all of that and never stopped doing it. It was 21 years of the Big Ticket that used to be Da Kid in Minnesota back in the 90's. For all it could remember, the game of basketball always had Kevin Garnett. However, for the first time since 1995, it would be without one of its fiercest and most fiery competitors.

Chapter 4: Garnett's Personal Life

Kevin Maurice Garnett is married to Brandi Padilla, who was his longtime girlfriend before getting married. They have been married since 2004. The marriage ceremony was the reason why Garnett was not able to suit up for Team USA in the Athens Olympics. The couple has a daughter together, and Kevin has defended the privacy of his family as much as he has defended the basket on the court.[xxxiii]

Garnett comes from a broken family. His mother Shirley and father O'Lewis never got married. He never became close with his father O'Lewis McCullough, but still gained his love for basketball from him. He has a stepfather, though, Ernest Irby. However, they never really got along because Ernest was never very supportive of Kevin's interest in basketball.

KG is tough on his teammates, but he was always one of the friendliest players in the NBA. Since joining the Timberwolves in 1995, he has become close friends with then-teammate and current head coach Sam Mitchell. He was also very close with Timberwolves teammate Malik Sealy who abruptly died after being involved in a car accident. As a tribute to the fallen Sealy, Garnett chose to wear the number 2 when he was traded to Brooklyn.[xxxiv]

Garnett maintains close ties with former players Tyron Lue and Paul Pierce, his teammate in Boston and Brooklyn. As Kevin never had a father figure in his life, he always looked up to his former head coach the late Flip Saunders. Flip would recount that KG always loved his teammates and would even want to let them stay with the team if he had the choice. Kevin also maintains a group of friends from his hometown in Mauldin. He calls this entourage the "Official Block Family."[xxxv]

Chapter 5: Garnett's Legacy and Impact on the Game

Kevin Garnett came into the NBA as an innovator. He was the first high school player to be drafted into the NBA since 1975. This paved the way for other players who went straight to the NBA from high school. Notable prep-to-pro players include Kobe Bryant, LeBron James, Amare Stoudemire, and Dwight Howard.

KG was a match-up nightmare. He came into the league where 7-footers would camp out in the paint to post up and wait for drop passes. Meanwhile, smaller centers and power forwards would typically bull their way to the basket using strength and athletic ability. Then, Kevin Garnett came along and entirely changed the power forward position and the role of 7-footers.

He was one of the first players to be called a "stretch 4," which is a power forward that can shoot the ball from the perimeter. He would shoot midrange jumpers and even sometimes three-pointers over the top of his defenders. When he was up against slower big men, Garnett, who is technically a 7-footer, would run and handle the ball like a guard and finish strong at the rim. At the same time, he would still defend the paint with his long arm span much like how typical 7-footers would do.

Garnett's innovative playing style gave tall but lanky players a chance to make it in the NBA. He is technically the prototype for players like Chris Bosh and LaMarcus Aldridge who are nearly 7-feet tall but would make their money and become All-Stars by shooting perimeter jumpers all day long. Standing at over 6'10", Kevin Durant handles the ball better than most guards and also shoots it above his defenders with ease, much like how KG used to do. However, no other player in the NBA draws more comparison to Kevin Garnett than Anthony Davis of the New Orleans Pelicans. Like Garnett, Davis was fond of playing point guard in his younger years before his growth spurt; hence Davis could handle and shoot the ball better than most big men. He also came into the league as a tall lanky guy but then grew up to be an elite paint defender who could run the floor with ease after a successful defensive play.

Above everything else, no other part of Garnett's ability as a basketball player has made a bigger impact than his ability to lead and mentor younger players. Coming to the Boston Celtics, Garnett would act as a mentor for not only the defensive oriented center Kendrick Perkins, but also for forwards Glen Davis and Jared Sullinger, both of whom are fond of shooting midrange jumpers.

KG also played the roles of both locker room and emotional leader for the Boston Celtics and would pump them up whenever they needed a boost of morale. Garnett would also take Brook Lopez of the Brooklyn Nets under his wing in his short stint in the state of New York. Currently, KG plays for the Minnesota Timberwolves but primarily acts as a mentor for young players such as Zach LaVine, Andrew Wiggins, and Karl-Anthony Towns. For the highly-touted Towns, who is a 7-footer and the top overall pick in the 2015 NBA Draft, he is fortunate to have come to the T-Wolves because nobody in the NBA is better suited to teach how to be a big man than the legendary Kevin Maurice Garnett.

No doubt Garnett is one of the best power forwards in the history of the game. He can even be argued to be the best in the position along with legends like Tim Duncan, Charles Barkley, Karl Malone, and Kevin McHale. And many players may try to emulate Kevin Garnett's brand of basketball. Some of them may even grow up to be a better shooter, better defender, or even an overall better basketball player. There are also other forwards and big men who have accomplished much more than what KG has done in his career. Make no mistake about it, though. No player will ever exceed the combination of skill, size, leadership, and fiery intensity that Kevin Garnett possesses.

Final Word/About the Author

I was born and raised in Norwalk, Connecticut. Growing up, I could often be found spending many nights watching basketball, soccer, and football matches with my father in the family living room. I love sports and everything that sports can embody. I believe that sports are one of most genuine forms of competition, heart, and determination. I write my works to learn more about influential athletes in the hopes that from my writing, you the reader can walk away inspired to put in an equal if not greater amount of hard work and perseverance to pursue your goals. If you enjoyed *Kevin Garnett: The Inspiring Story of One of Basketball's Greatest Power Forwards*, please leave a review! Also, you can read more of my works on *Rob Gronkowski*, *Brett Favre*, *Calvin Johnson*, *Drew Brees*, *J.J. Watt*, *Colin Kaepernick*, *Aaron Rodgers*, *Peyton Manning*, *Tom Brady*, *Russell Wilson*, *Michael Jordan*, *LeBron James*, *Kyrie Irving*, *Klay Thompson*, *Stephen Curry*, *Kevin Durant*, *Russell Westbrook*, *Anthony Davis*, *Chris Paul*, *Blake Griffin*, *Kobe Bryant*, *Joakim Noah*, *Scottie Pippen*, *Carmelo Anthony*, *Kevin Love*, *Grant Hill*, *Tracy McGrady*, *Vince Carter*, *Patrick Ewing*, *Karl Malone*, *Tony Parker*, *Allen Iverson*, *Hakeem Olajuwon*, *Reggie Miller*, *Michael Carter-Williams*, *John Wall*, *James Harden*, *Tim Duncan*, *Steve Nash*, *Draymond Green*, *Kawhi*

Leonard, Dwyane Wade, Ray Allen, Pau Gasol, Dirk Nowitzki, Jimmy Butler, Paul Pierce, Manu Ginobili, Pete Maravich, Larry Bird, Kyle Lowry, Jason Kidd, David Robinson, LaMarcus Aldridge, Derrick Rose, Paul George, Chris Paul and Marc Gasol in the Kindle Store. If you love basketball, check out my website at claytongeoffreys.com to join my exclusive list where I let you know about my latest books and give you lots of goodies.

Like what you read? Please leave a review!

I write because I love sharing the stories of influential people like Kevin Garnett with fantastic readers like you. My readers inspire me to write more so please do not hesitate to let me know what you thought by leaving a review! If you love books on life, basketball, or productivity, check out my website at claytongeoffreys.com to join my exclusive list where I let you know about my latest books. Aside from being the first to hear about my latest releases, you can also download a free copy of *33 Life Lessons: Success Principles, Career Advice & Habits of Successful People*. See you there!

Clayton

References

[i] Beck Howard. "A Man in Full: An Oral History of Kevin Garnett, the Player Who Changed the NBA." *Bleacher Report.* 15 May 2015. Web.

[ii] *Jockbio.com.* Black Book Partners, 2010. Web.

[iii] *Jockbio.com.* Black Book Partners, 2010. Web.

[iv] Carter, Bob. "'Da Kid' Progressed Quickly. *ESPN Classic.* ESPN. Web.

[v] *Jockbio.com.* Black Book Partners, 2010. Web.

[vi] Carter, Bob. "'Da Kid' Progressed Quickly. *ESPN Classic.* ESPN. Web.

[vii] *Jockbio.com.* Black Book Partners, 2010. Web.

[viii] Peters, Austin. "What Made Kevin Garnett So Special Coming Out of High School". *Fan Sided.* 9 March, 2016. Web

[ix] Beck Howard. "A Man in Full: An Oral History of Kevin Garnett, the Player Who Changed the NBA." *Bleacher Report.* 15 May 2015. Web.

[x] Lex. "Laettner Calls Out Flip over Garnett". *Lex Nihil Novi.* 20 February 1996. Web.

[xi] Carter, Bob. "'Da Kid' Progressed Quickly. *ESPN Classic.* ESPN. Web.

[xii] Carter, Bob. "'Da Kid' Progressed Quickly. *ESPN Classic.* ESPN. Web.

[xiii] Beck Howard. "A Man in Full: An Oral History of Kevin Garnett, the Player Who Changed the NBA." *Bleacher Report.* 15 May 2015. Web.

[xiv] Beck Howard. "A Man in Full: An Oral History of Kevin Garnett, the Player Who Changed the NBA." *Bleacher Report.* 15 May 2015. Web.

[xv] *Jockbio.com.* Black Book Partners, 2010. Web.

[xvi] Beck Howard. "A Man in Full: An Oral History of Kevin Garnett, the Player Who Changed the NBA." *Bleacher Report.* 15 May 2015. Web.

[xvii] "Garnett Named League's MVP". *NBA.* 3 May 2004. Web.

[xviii] Gaines, Cork. "How Kevin Garnet Made $327 Million to Become

the Highest-Paid Player in NBA History". *Business Insider.* 13 July 2015. Web.

[xix] Beck Howard. "A Man in Full: An Oral History of Kevin Garnett, the Player Who Changed the NBA." *Bleacher Report.* 15 May 2015. Web.

[xx] Beck Howard. "A Man in Full: An Oral History of Kevin Garnett, the Player Who Changed the NBA." *Bleacher Report.* 15 May 2015. Web.

[xxi] Beck Howard. "A Man in Full: An Oral History of Kevin Garnett, the Player Who Changed the NBA." *Bleacher Report.* 15 May 2015. Web.

[xxii] Gaines, Cork. "How Kevin Garnet Made $327 Million to Become the Highest-Paid Player in NBA History". *Business Insider.* 13 July 2015. Web.

[xxiii] Beck Howard. "A Man in Full: An Oral History of Kevin Garnett, the Player Who Changed the NBA." *Bleacher Report.* 15 May 2015. Web.

[xxiv] Beck Howard. "A Man in Full: An Oral History of Kevin Garnett, the Player Who Changed the NBA." *Bleacher Report.* 15 May 2015. Web.

[xxv] Beck Howard. "A Man in Full: An Oral History of Kevin Garnett, the Player Who Changed the NBA." *Bleacher Report.* 15 May 2015. Web.

[xxvi] Gaines, Cork. "How Kevin Garnet Made $327 Million to Become the Highest-Paid Player in NBA History". *Business Insider.* 13 July 2015. Web.

[xxvii] Mazzeo, Mike. "Nets face record $80 million luxury-tax bill". *ESPN.* 3 July 2013. Web.

[xxviii] "Kevin Garnett Returns to Minnesota". *ESPN.* 20 January 2015. Web.

[xxix] Beck Howard. "A Man in Full: An Oral History of Kevin Garnett, the Player Who Changed the NBA." *Bleacher Report.* 15 May 2015. Web.

[xxx] Beck Howard. "A Man in Full: An Oral History of Kevin Garnett, the Player Who Changed the NBA." *Bleacher Report.* 15 May 2015. Web.

[xxxi] Hartwell, Darrent. "Kevin Garnett Pays Powerful Tribute to Flip

Saunders on Facebook." *NESN*. 25 October 2015. Web

[xxxii] Hartwell, Darren. "Kevin Garnett: Tutoring Wolves Like Putting Puppies In Box, Shaking It (Video)". *NESN*. 12 November 2015. Web.

[xxxiii] *Fabwags*. 6 May 2014. Web.

[xxxiv] "Garnett to war No. 2 to Honor Sealy". *ESPN*. 19 July 2013. Web.

[xxxv] Montville, Leigh. "Still the Kid". *Sports on Earth*. 30 October 2012. Web.